DIABETES CONTROL
and
THE KOSHER DIET

by Ada P. Kahn, M.P.H.

WORDSCOPE ASSOCIATES
SKOKIE, ILLINOIS

For information, contact: WORDSCOPE ASSOCIATES
P. O. Box 1594
Skokie, Illinois 60077
U.S.A.

International Standard Book Number 0-930121-00-7

Library of Congress Card Catalog Number 84-051535

Other books
by Ada P. Kahn, M.P.H.

Help Yourself To Health series (1983):
ARTHRITIS
DIABETES
HEADACHES
HIGH BLOOD PRESSURE

Contents

Acknowledgments

The author is grateful to Melvin M. Chertack, M.D., F.A.C.P., for expressing the need for this book, and for his assistance in editing the medical aspects of the manuscript. His recommendations for discussion of specific concerns of patients regarding health and religion contribute to the readability of DIABETES CONTROL and THE KOSHER DIET.

Further, the author is grateful to Rabbi Dr. Norman Berlat, Vice-president, Chicago Rabbinical Council, whose careful consideration of the religious aspects of good health makes this book a good source for brief answers to frequently asked questions. His patience and guidance throughout all stages of preparation of the manuscript are appreciated.

Additionally, the author thanks Rabbis Shlomo Rapoport, Nathan I. Weiss, and Benjamin Shandalov, of the Chicago Rabbinical Council, for their encouragement, cooperation and assistance. Each rabbi independently reviewed the manuscript. After each review, in rabbinic style, the three met with the author to discuss further possibilities for elucidation of certain points.

All who participated in preparation of DIABETES CONTROL and THE KOSHER DIET appreciate the contribution of Rabbi Oscar Z. Fasman, who reviewed the manuscript and clarified certain aspects regarding matters of Kashrut.

The author thanks Teila Fefferman Lichtman for her assistance in developing the recipes and serving suggestions included in the book. Thanks to her husband, Heshey, and their children, Zahava and Ben Zion, and their Grandma Rhoda for much patience and good humor during the many hours while Teila was in the kitchen!

Thanks also to Teila for providing useful information on ethnic nutritional customs. The handbook, *Chicago's Ethnic Populations: Nutritional Dimensions,* published in 1980 by the Chicago Dietetic Association, Inc., was a helpful resource.

Rabbi Eliezer Lederfeind, Brooklyn, NY, a founder of the Association of Jewish Diabetics, provided helpful insights about the concerns of potential readers.

Rabbi Elyahu Safran, Pittsburgh, provided useful material regarding hospitalized Jewish patients.

Dr. Earl Auerbach, Charles R. McLaughlin and Abraham Adler provided counsel and assistance in preparing the sections of the book concerning kosher meat.

Ruth D. Kahn provided a valuable contribution as a research assistant.

Michael Kite provided editorial assistance.

Toby S. Stern, R.D., provided an audit of the nutritive values noted in the recipes.

Art work by James N. Lambert
Typography and Assembly by Tracy R. Butler and Dennis J. Zider

FOREWORD

One of my Orthodox Jewish patients was having some difficulty with her diabetic dietary management. "But Doctor," she said, "with all of your recommendations about foods and the dietary education you have given me, I cannot find a handy reference that explains how to control my diabetes with diet and also conform to the rules of *Kashrut*. Is there such a book?"

This book by Ada P. Kahn is that handy guidebook for which my patients—and many others—have been waiting. In her easy-to-read style, Ada has compiled a basic reference that fulfills this long-neglected area of health care in the Jewish community (as well as for many who love kosher cooking).

It took me many years to realize that a good reason for some patients' failures to comply with the recommended Exchange Lists diet was the lack of material integrating religious tradition.

I was raised in an Orthodox home, have had many years of teaching and treating patients with dietary needs and consider myself a very practical clinician and educator. Yet this one patient's comment dramatically reminded me of my frustration with doctors and dietitians who counsel kosher patients about diets without explaining how to implement recommendations and coordinate them with the kosher diet.

This handbook about the basics of diabetes control and the kosher diet will be useful to patients and also to health professionals and institutions who care for patients who observe the laws of *Kashrut*. Physicians and dietitians can augment their patient education programs by recommending that Jewish patients read and use this handy compilation of information.

Ada P. Kahn and I began talking about the need for this book even before she completed her earlier book, *DIABETES*, one of four in the "Help Yourself To Health" series published in 1983 by Contemporary Books, Inc., Chicago, Illinois. As I reviewed that manuscript in the capacity as her medical consultant and wrote the foreword for that book, we mentally made notes for inclusions in *this* book.

While her earlier book is a good basic introduction for understanding diabetes and learning how to keep good control, it does not address the special concerns of kosher patients which are featured in this new book.

This book specifically presents the relationship of diabetes management and the kosher diet, a topic which at this time we believe has never been addressed in book form. The author conferred with Rabbi Dr. Norman Berlat and his colleagues at the Chicago Rabbinical Council to assure that material in this book is religiously—as well as medically—accurate.

To be sure that the recipes and serving suggestions in this book meet the "taste test," Ada enlisted the assistance of a modern kosher homemaker and dietitian, Ms. Teila Lichtman, R.D., whose experience includes counseling kosher diabetic patients as well as Jewish patients from a variety of ethnic backgrounds. All involved in preparation of this book agree that the serving suggestions are *meicholim*!

Dietary control is recommended not only for the diabetic, but for all persons who want to control the "waist diseases," such as obesity, high blood pressure, heart disease, and arthritis. By integrating patients' diets with their religious beliefs, we can broaden their perspectives regarding what they eat and help them conform to dietary recommendations.

This book is presented with the hope that it will encourage better understanding of the kosher diet as well as diabetes, encourage patients following the laws of Kashrut to eat more intelligently and motivate them to better health.

Further, we hope that this book will lead to pleasanter experience in kosher eating and a better relationship between health care and spiritual sanctity. For the best health care, physical, emotional and spiritual balance must be maintained. We hope this book will lead to such fulfillment for many readers.

Melvin M. Chertack, M.D., F.A.C.P.
Past President
Northern Illinois Affiliate
American Diabetes Association

FOREWORD

The Halachic principles of the Torah are the guideposts of Jewish life and experience. Within the realm of Jewish law the individual is provided with the spectrum of the totality of human behavior and the method of seeing that such behavior is in consonance with the requirements of Torah-True Judaism.

Two such Torah laws addressed by this unusual manual are the Jewish Dietary Laws of Kashrut and one's responsibility to properly care for his or her own body.

Kosher food is salutory for both body and soul. The laws of Kashrut are complex and Ada P. Kahn has devoted much time consulting with experts in this field to produce a book for Jewish diabetics that will meet not only their dietary requirements but also will be in total keeping with the principles and practices of Halacha as it pertains to Kashrut.

Likewise, G-d requires that each individual properly care for his or her body which has been entrusted as a Divine gift. Diabetes requires that special care and consideration be taken in the preparation and measurement of food as well as following specific guidelines of one's physician and dietitian.

This outstanding book will be helpful to the diabetic individual in preparing tasty and nutritious kosher meals. The wide variety of kosher recipes provided by Teila Fefferman Lichtman, R.D. will certainly please the palate as well as add variety to daily, Sabbath and holiday meals.

Readers should remember that all ingredients mentioned in this book (whether or not specifically identified) must be rabbinically certified as kosher. All Passover ingredients must be certified kosher for Passover, as explained by Ms. Kahn in the chapter on holidays and serving suggestions.

Everyday Jewish life encompasses social functions in the synagogue, many of which involve food. Often, diabetics and others on controlled diets are implored by friends and relatives to "take a little something." DIABETES CONTROL and THE KOSHER DIET will help others understand the basis for the diabetic's controlled diet and the necessity for carefully maintaining their diet at all times.

In addition to friends and relatives of the kosher diabetic, it will be helpful to physicians and dietitians who want more details on Kashrut in Jewish life.

I wish to express my personal gratitude to Rabbis Oscar Z. Fasman, Shlomo Rapoport, Nathan I. Weiss and Benjamin Shandalov of the Chicago Rabbinical Council for their generous gifts of time in reviewing the manuscript of this book with the author and myself. I am grateful for their helpful guidance and suggestions which have greatly enhanced the accuracy of the Jewish content of DIABETES CONTROL and THE KOSHER DIET.

This handy guidebook will enable Jewish diabetics to more fully enjoy the blessings of *Gutte Ma'acholim* and good health.

> Rabbi Dr. Norman Berlat
> Vice-President
> Chicago Rabbinical Council

Introduction

You probably picked up this book because your doctor told you that you have diabetes or that someone in your family has diabetes.

This is an introductory guidebook for the individual who has diabetes and observes the laws of Kashrut. It is also intended for family members of "kosher diabetics." Additionally, this book should be helpful to physicians, dietitians and others involved in the care of diabetic patients who follow the laws of Kashrut.

You may already know that with diabetes careful attention to diet is necessary. Like thousands of others who follow the rules of Kashrut, you probably have many questions about how to observe your dietary practices and at the same time prepare, serve, or eat food appropriate for good control of diabetes.

Whether your diabetes was recently diagnosed or you have lived with it for a long time, this book will be helpful because you will learn more about the importance of controlling your diabetes, new ways to prepare kosher foods and modify your daily eating habits. With this information, you will increase your chances for better control of diabetes.

You CAN observe the rules of Kashrut and maintain a good diet for controlling diabetes. Observing the dietary laws means following Torah principles and a lifestyle that relates to every aspect of what, when, where and how you eat. Your choice of food and certain limitations on selection of food, meal planning and combinations of foods, and eating away from home are all influenced by your commitment to the rules of Kashrut.

Now that you want to improve your own health or the health of one you love through appropriate dietary control, you will want to make further modifications in your daily activities to incorporate this essential additional dimension in your everyday planning: a *healthful* kosher diet for the control of diabetes.

In addition to giving you some guidelines on kosher cooking for the individual with diabetes, this book will help you understand the basics about diabetes, what it is, how it can be controlled, why exercise, rest and careful supervision by a physician are essential.

Many holidays and festivals among Jewish people center around specially prepared foods. For many, however, eating certain foods in certain quantities can be harmful to health and a threat to life. This is true for many people who have diabetes. In this book you will find new ways to prepare some familiar foods for holidays that can be served appetizingly to the person who has diabetes as well as to others in the family.

Eating habits strongly affect our health. The old saying, "you are what you eat," isn't just a *bubbeh meiseh* (grandmother's tale); it is a fact of life and health. What we eat has an important influence on how we feel, what diseases we get, and how we cope with illness. Of course, heredity plays a part, too. But what and how we eat to some extent may modify the effects of heredity.

In few other diseases does what we eat play as important a role as it does in diabetes. In many cases, diabetes can be controlled with only slight modifications in eating habits. In other cases, good diabetes management also requires the use of insulin injections or oral medication taken under a physician's careful supervision. Yet diabetes is a disease that if uncontrolled, can be a serious threat to life.

When you first learned that you have diabetes you may have been frightened. However, you may not have been completely surprised to learn that you have it if your parents or others in the family have it now or at one time had it. A tendency toward diabetes is often inherited. But, while diabetes does run in families, it is NOT contagious.

Some physicians say that diabetes is more common among Jewish people of Ashkenazic origin (from eastern Europe) than Jewish people from other parts of the world. No one knows why. Perhaps diet plays a role. However, diabetes is by no means a "Jewish" disease. About one in every four families in the United

States has someone with diabetes. That's about one out of every 20 individuals adding up to an estimated 10 million people.

Why do people get diabetes?

Doctors and researchers aren't sure why some individuals get diabetes and others don't. But they do know that hundreds of thousands of individuals with diabetes live with their disease and lead happy lives. New treatments for diabetes have contributed to healthier lives for many people who have diabetes.

Controlling your diabetes is largely up to you. You will want to follow advice given to you by your physician, nurse, dietitian and others on your health care team. If what you hear from your health care team is ever in conflict with what you read in this book, bring your questions to them. They know your individual condition best. Should your question involve Kashrut as opposed to a strictly medical matter, ask your Orthodox rabbi.

As the saying goes, you can't pick your relatives. You can't change your heredity. But you CAN choose your friends. Make your best friend a healthier lifestyle and a modified diet.

In this guidebook, you'll learn how to begin modifying the kosher diet when your own precious good health or the health of one you love is endangered by diabetes.

L'chayim! (To life!).

Diabetes And The Kosher Diet

Diabetes is unlike many illnesses. Diabetes is not a disease for which your physician will simply give you a prescription and ask you to return for another visit in a month.

Treating diabetes requires close cooperation on your part and a commitment from you just as large as your commitment to the observance of Kashrut. Your participation in the treatment includes following your physician's close supervision, giving careful attention to your diet, perhaps losing weight, exercising more, changing your smoking or drinking habits, and possibly using insulin injections or oral medications that lower the blood sugar.

Individuals who have diabetes at certain stages of life need special care. For example, females who have diabetes during their childbearing years and who are considering having a baby need special care before and during pregnancy to put themselves in the best condition for delivering a healthy, normal infant. Older adults require particular attention to good eating habits as additional illnesses may complicate their control of diabetes.

In this book, you will learn about a variety of aspects of traditional kosher cooking that can be modified to provide a better diet for controlling diabetes for individuals of all ages. For example, you will learn to prepare food with less fat, less salt, and more fiber. You will learn about the importance of weight control and how to incorporate recipes for your favorite foods into your daily individualized meal plans as recommended by your physician and dietitian.

In Jewish households, Sabbath and holidays are times for families and friends to come together for special meals. After you read this book, you can feel confident about serving a meal to an individual with diabetes, the dietary requirements, and appropriate recipes for appetizing kosher foods that can be enjoyed by all.

In this book, all ingredients used in recipes (Chapter 6) must be rabbinically certified as kosher. All ingredients for Passover foods must be certified kosher for Passover.

What is Kosher cooking?

Kosher cooks have many different ways of preparing foods. Your mother, mother-in-law and grandmothers may have their own unique ways to make chopped liver, chicken soup, gefilte fish or latkes. How people cook depends largely on where they grew up and where they learned to cook. In many parts of the world, Jewish people used all parts of the animal, including the neck, lining of the intestines (to make kishke), calves' feet for *pchah* (aspic), the liver, lung, stomach, and bones in soup as flavoring.

A large number of traditional European dishes are based on starch, such as potatoes or noodles because those dishes were plentiful and inexpensive in European countries. Beets seem to be one of the few vegetables found in many traditional recipes (borscht); vegetables were not always abundant in Europe.

Historically, the kosher diet has been high in fat. Many cuts of kosher meat are well-marbled, and generations thought, perhaps rightfully so, that the fat content contributed to the special mouth-watering flavors.

Schmaltz (rendered chicken fat) has been a favorite ingredient for many traditional Jewish dishes. It has been used for flavor and even as an ingredient for sandwiches. Have you ever tasted pumpernickel bread spread with schmaltz and covered with thin slices of garlic and/or onion? Your taste remembrance will help you understand how this tradition came about. (Umm!) In recent years, modern kosher cooks have become aware of the role of fat in heart diseases and have cut down on overall fats and have decreased the amount of schmaltz used in cooking. Instead, they use *pareve* (neutral; containing no milk or meat ingredients) margarine or kosher certified vegetable oil.

Fried dishes also have been popular in kosher cooking. *Blintzes* (crepes) and *matzo brie* (fried matzo) are favorites in many

Jewish households. Instead of using schmaltz or butter, many cooks now use small amounts of vegetable oil.

Schmaltz has been a "staple" of the kosher diet for as far back as anyone remembers. If you are preparing food for a person who has diabetes or high blood pressure, you will want to learn to make substitutions for schmaltz.

Many traditional kosher foods are also high in sodium (salt). Remember how thirsty you can get after eating herring or salted lox? Reducing your salt intake is important for preventing and controlling high blood pressure. (High blood pressure can make treating your diabetes even more difficult.)

Additionally, the koshering process is a salting process, and in general, kosher meats and poultry may tend to be somewhat high in sodium. Fresh kosher fish, on the other hand, does not have to be salted to be kosher. (A list of kosher cuts of meat and kosher fish appears in Chapter 3.)

Jewish people from different parts of the world bring with them a variety of traditional eating habits. For example, some recent Russian Jewish immigrants in many American cities seem to use more fat in food preparation than many American Jewish cooks. Many Russians use a lot of garlic and green onions for seasoning cooked meat and chicken.

Foods with a high salt content, such as herring, sauerkraut, pickled beets, sausage, caviar and olives are popular with some Russian Jews. Russians have traditionally eaten good sources of fiber, such as black bread, kasha (a type of buckwheat), raw fruits and raw vegetables.

Some Russian Jewish immigrants have a tendency to become overweight and their extra weight has led to the development of diabetes, high blood pressure and other problems. Some dietitians have found that many recent Russian Jewish immigrants have various misconceptions about diet and diabetes. For example, some think that black bread is good but white bread, rice and macaroni make "your sugar rise." Some think that potatoes should be soaked overnight to remove the starch.

Others think that raw cabbage is helpful in reducing blood sugar. Physicians say there is no scientific evidence that these notions have any medical validity. But who is to argue? After all, many Jewish mothers believe strongly in chicken soup as a cure-all for everything from colds to disappointment in love!

Regardless of the evidence, doctors and dietitians often face many varying attitudes from different ethnic groups when explaining the importance of diet in the control of diabetes.

Some Russian Jewish eating traditions are maintained even though the families are in America. For example, in the larger American cities, extended families often live in the same neighborhood, or perhaps in the same apartment building. In some cases the grandmother will care for the children while both parents work or attend English classes.

Grandmothers all over the world are known for emphasizing eating. *Ess, mein kind!* (Eat, my child!). Thus many children are encouraged to eat often and often too much.

At family gatherings among Jewish people, regardless of ethnic background, large quantities of many different foods usually are prepared and served. It is common for guests to bring appealing and tasty dishes to put on the table; these may include fried and fatty meats and rich cakes. This display of attractive, rich foods needs a few dishes lower in calories and fat. Learn to include dishes appropriate for the family member or a visitor with diabetes.

Adapting kosher cooking for better diabetes control

In Chapter 6, 7, and 8 you will find recipes for some of the familiar kosher foods prepared in ways that are appropriate for helping to control diabetes. Additionally, you will find recipes for foods that will add tasty and healthful dimensions to your traditional meals. You will also find some new ideas for meal planning for holidays, the Sabbath, and everyday meals.

In Chapter 5 you will learn about the Exchange Lists for diabetic meal planning. These lists present a way to help you to control the glucose levels in your blood by showing you the proper amounts and kinds of foods to eat each day. Examples on the Exchange Lists indicate kosher foods and include no *traif* (non-kosher foods).

In your *bubbeh's* (grandmother's) day, keeping kosher, providing variety for everyone in the family and planning appropriate meals for a person with diabetes may have been a large assignment. Now, however, many kosher foods are conveniently prepared by commercial food companies and are nutritious, tasty and appropriate for individuals with diabetes.

Serving good meals for everyone now can be easier with occasional use of kosher "convenience" foods that are available at your local kosher food store. In the chapter on "Kosher Convenience Foods" you will learn how to find out about the calorie, carbohydrate and fat content of many prepared foods, and how to include them in the daily food plan for the individual who has diabetes. Information on obtaining the Kosher Directory of commercially prepared foods is also given.

What about eating out? What can you eat in a kosher restaurant? Can you keep kosher, travel and follow an appropriate diet for controlling diabetes? Should you carry certain foods or food items with you? These and other questions will be answered in the chapter on Traveling, Sick Days and Special Care.

Getting acquainted with the observance of Kashrut

Because this book will be read by physicians, nurses, dietitians and social workers who are not familiar with kosher dietary rules but must make appropriate recommendations to patients with diabetes, Chapter 3 gives the basic outlines of Kashrut rules. This section is not intended to be the "last word" on what is kosher and what is not. For the observant Jew, this chapter will look like the *aleph-bais* (a, b, c's). If you have questions regarding combining Kashrut observances and dietary habits for good control of diabetes, talk with your Orthodox rabbi.

Learning more about diabetes

As you learn about diabetes and controlling the disease with a good and healthy kosher diet, appropriate exercise and rest and perhaps insulin or oral medication, you will probably want to read more about diabetes. There are many books and periodicals available to help keep you up-to-date on research on diabetes, new products of interest to those with the disease and organizations to help you keep in touch with others who live successfully with their disease under control. These publications and sources are listed and described in the chapter on "Resources."

Knowing more about the meaning of words relating to diabetes can help you understand the importance of what your physician and health care team tell you during visits to your health center. In the Word List you will find many words pertaining to nutrition, diabetes, and food preparation that can help you follow your physician's directions, live with the laws of Kashrut and diabetes, and feel well.

Ess gesundterheit and shalom! (Eat with good health and peace!)

Understanding Diabetes

Your physician or dietitian may have explained the basics about diabetes to you. Or, you may know about diabetes because another family member has it. Whether you know about diabetes or if the disease is new to you, a review of some of the basics will help you understand why modifying your food preparation and eating habits is so important.

Perhaps you forgot to ask many questions when your doctor explained diabetes to you. The information in this chapter will help you answer some of the questions you still have after your last visit to your physician's office.

Why does diabetes happen, and why did it happen to you or a family member?

Diabetes occurs when your body is not able to use the foods you eat appropriately as a result of not enough or inappropriate use of insulin in your body. What is insulin? Insulin is a substance that is made naturally by the body to help produce energy from the carbohydrates and sugars in food. If the body does not make enough insulin, diabetes mellitus (sometimes known as sugar diabetes) may develop.

Food you eat is changed in your body to glucose, a form of sugar, which your cells utilize as a source of energy. Glucose causes your blood glucose level to rise. This in turn starts the release of a hormone called insulin from a gland in the abdomen known as the pancreas.

Insulin is important because it regulates the level of glucose in your blood. Insulin also aids the utilization and storage of glucose in your body. If you have diabetes, you may not produce any insulin at all or perhaps just not enough to help the glucose from your blood transfer into appropriate ·cells. If your own supply of insulin is not adequate, glucose will not be used by your cells and will build up in your blood. You may have heard the phrase, "too much sugar in the blood," or "too much sugar in the urine." When people say this, they really mean too much glucose. This condition can only be determined by tests your physician will do or simple tests you can do at home. (Self-monitoring techniques will be mentioned in Chapter 11.)

There is much confusion regarding words people use to describe diabetes. For example, *diabetes* is really short for the term *diabetes mellitus,* which was derived from the Greek words meaning "passing through" and "sweet as honey." *Diabetes mellitus* applies to the condition when there is an excess of sugar in the blood and/or urine. In this book, the word *diabetes* refers to *diabetes mellitus,* the disease you may have heard people call "too much sugar."

There is another type of diabetes known as *diabetes insipidus.* In that disease, there is an excess of fluid loss by the body. This book is not about diabetes insipidus. If you are concerned about that condition, ask your physician or librarian for other reading materials.

Diabetes: Your neighbor's and yours

If you talk about diabetes with a friend or neighbor, you may become confused, because no two cases are exactly alike. You may want to talk about the differences in kosher recipes with your friends, but when it comes to medical questions, talk to your doctor!

There are several types of diabetes and within these types, the disease can be very different. Your doctor may tell you that you have Type I or Type II, or that you are insulin-dependent or non-insulin dependent. The best way to understand the differences between types of diabetes is to know how the American Diabetes Association classifies the disease: (see chart on p. 10)

Type I. Type I is insulin-dependent. Although it most commonly occurs before adulthood, it begins at all ages. Some doctors still may call this type of diabetes "juvenile diabetes." It affects about one of every 2,500 children in whom the pancreas produces little or no insulin and the patients are dependent on outside sources of insulin. Before the discovery of insulin in 1921, many children with insulin-dependent diabetes did not live long. Now, however, the disease can be well controlled with insulin, appropriate diet and exercise, and regular monitoring.

Type II. Type II diabetes is much more common than Type I. Type II is non-insulin-dependent diabetes. In this form of the disease, additional insulin is not usually required to sustain life. This type usually occurs in middle or older age and frequently in overweight people. Very often this type of diabetes can be controlled effectively by modifications in the diet, exercise and possibly oral medication.

According to the American Diabetes Association, Type II diabetes affects about 90 percent of the 11 million diabetics in the United States, including about five million victims who have not been diagnosed. About 600,000 cases are diagnosed each year; countless others go undetected.

The American Diabetes Association estimates that 60 to 90 percent of those with non-insulin-dependent diabetes in western societies are obese, so you can see the importance of easing up on the "schmaltz" you eat.

Non-insulin-dependent diabetes used to be called "maturity-onset diabetes" and your doctor still may call it that. Type II (non-insulin-dependent) is much more common than Type I (Insulin-dependent). This type is less severe than insulin-dependent diabetes and starts more slowly. With both types of diabetes, careful diet control and weight control are necessary.

Like opinions from scholarly rabbis, there are even more sides to the story about types of diabetes. One, called "gestational diabetes," applies only to diabetes that develops during pregnancy. Also, diabetes can be associated with use of certain drugs or chemicals. And, diabetes can be secondary to diseases of the pancreas or endocrine system. These types are not discussed in this book. If you want details about them, ask your physician for reference materials. However, the dietary needs may be the same and this book may be helpful.

To better understand the differences between Type I and Type II diabetes, please refer to the chart below. It will give you a better picture of when it occurs, how it is noticed, whether family history is relevant, what treatment is used, and whether obesity is a factor.

INSULIN-DEPENDENDENT and
NON-INSULIN-DEPENDENT DIABETES

	Insulin-Dependent TYPE I	Non-Insulin-Dependent TYPE II
Age of onset	Usually during youth, but can occur at any age.	Usually during adulthood; more common in older people.
How noticed	Usually appears abruptly and progresses rapidly.	Gradual in onset; the disease may go unnoticed for years.
Symptoms	Frequent urination Increased thirst Unusual hunger Weight loss Irritability Weakness and fatigue Nausea and vomiting	Excess weight Drowsiness Blurred vision Tingling and numbness in hands and feet Skin infections Slow healing of cuts (especially on the feet) Itching
Family background	Diabetes not always present in other family members.	Often diabetes was present in other family members.
Treatment	Insulin injections are necessary. Diet, exercise and emotional control are necessary.	Insulin injections are not always necessary. Oral medications are sometimes recommended. Diet, exercise and emotional control are necessary.
Complications	Problems affecting blood vessels, eyes, kidneys, and nerves may occur at any age.	Problems affecting blood vessels, eyes, kidneys, and nerves may occur at any age.
Related to obesity	Not necessarily.	80 percent of all patients are overweight at the time of diagnosis.

What are the symptoms?

Symptoms of diabetes vary between individuals. You may have noticed increased thirst, excessive urination, increased appetite and loss of weight, itchy skin, or that sores and cuts healed slowly, that you tired easily and became drowsy often, or had impaired vision.

However, if you've discussed diabetes with your friends and neighbors, you know that in the early stages, many people do not notice any symptoms. Many older adults who have diabetes have only a vague feeling of not being well. In those persons, the physician detects the disease with a blood sugar test after noticing glucose in the urine. Further tests confirm the diagnosis.

Your physician will want to use a combination of tests to diagnose and monitor your diabetes. As you progress in your treatment your physician will re-evaluate your treatment plan frequently because your blood sugar level changes in response to your diet, amount of exercise, type and amount of medication, and emotional stress you face.

Using modern diagnostic and testing procedures, your physician can help you control your diabetes in medical ways while you work to control it in dietary ways.

How is diabetes treated?

For non-insulin dependent diabetes, diet is the most important part of treatment. However, if your blood sugar level cannot be controlled by diet and exercise alone, a blood sugar reducing therapy will be prescribed for you.

For insulin-dependent diabetes, your physician will prescribe insulin in an injectable form as well as a special diet and exercise program to go along with your modified kosher diet and lifestyle. Your physician may prescribe oral medication if he/she believes that it will be helpful for you. Your individual case will determine which type of therapy will be best.

Whether you use injected insulin or oral medication, it is essential that you follow your physician's instructions regarding diet. Your physician's treatment goal is to preserve your own insulin output as much as possible. You can help reach this goal by complying with the diet specially recommended for you, getting your weight down to your ideal level and taking your medication or injecting your insulin as it is prescribed for you.

If your doctor wants you to use insulin, he or she will review with you the various types available, determine the dose that best meets your needs, and explain when and how to do your injections. For example, you may be advised to take the insulin about one-half hour before breakfast or before the evening meal, or occasionally before other meals or bedtime.

Human insulin is made from the body's building blocks called amino acids. Most insulin now used to treat diabetes comes from the pancreas of cattle and hogs. Artificially produced human insulin is also available. Various types of insulins differ chemically and differ from insulin made by the human pancreas. All types of insulin are proteins.

Is insulin kosher?

All insulin for human injection, regardless of its source, is ritually permissible. Are you wondering how anything derived from hogs can be consumed by a religious Jew? First, when insulin is prepared, it is in itself not edible, and even "a dog will not eat it," the test in Halachah of when non-kosher food is no longer forbidden. With the development of human insulin, however, the need to use pork insulin has been reduced.

Secondly, there is a Hebrew term, *Pikuach Nefesh* (rescuing a life). This term denotes an injunction to set aside other considerations when someone's life is endangered. The concept is rooted in a warning in the Torah (the Jewish law) not to "stand idly by the blood of thy neighbor." The duty of saving life even overrides Sabbath laws. The law applies in cases of persons critically ill or those faced with possible danger to life, such as individuals with diabetes. The underlying idea is that God's commandments were given to man so that he should LIVE by them, not die in their performance.

If you are one of many people who need to use injected insulin, you will have help in learning to do so. Your health care team, consisting of your physician, a nurse, and usually a dietitian, will assist you in learning to inject insulin, the importance of rotating the site of injection, what to expect in the way of reactions and how to avoid them.

Diabetic emergencies

Although insulin reactions are not usual, they do happen and you should know how to recognize reactions and how to take care of yourself. For example, your doctor may advise you to carry carbohydrate and protein sources to eat before you exercise or work strenuously and to keep quick sources of carbohydrates, such as fruit drinks containing sugar, handy. Several kosher quick sugar products are available that you can carry in your purse or pocket. Also, your doctor may tell you about glucagon therapy to treat insulin shock.

Oral medications

Diabetes medication also comes in pills which lower blood sugar levels. In most cases of non-insulin-dependent diabetes, the basis of treatment is diet and oral drugs (as well as insulin); drugs are usually prescribed only AFTER diet therapy alone has not been effective. However, in some cases, the pills can be used as the person is losing weight and medical conditions require reducing blood sugar.

In addition to regular use of your injected insulin or oral medication, a good healthy diet and an everyday exercise program, a sound mental outlook will help you control your diabetes.

Now that you know a little more about diabetes and the importance of diet in controlling the disease, you are ready to review the basics of the kosher diet, good nutrition and the Exchange List system of kosher meal planning for good diabetes control.

DIABETIC EMERGENCIES
For Those With Insulin-Dependent Diabetes

**KETOACIDOSIS
(DIABETIC COMA)**

This is a condition in which blood sugar is elevated. Muscle and fat break down and disturb the acid-alkaline balance in the body. Lack of consciousness or coma results.

This occurs because of insufficient insulin while there is stress in the body (physical or emotional), infection or serious illness.

Symptoms should be recognized and treated quickly.

Symptoms may include flushed, dry skin, drowsiness, a fruity breath odor, deep labored breathing, vomiting and abdominal pain.

**HYPOGLYCEMIA
(LOW BLOOD SUGAR)**

This is a condition in which there is an excess of insulin, too much exercise, or not enough food.

Avoid this complication by self-monitoring of urine or blood. Adjust your combination of insulin, food and exercise.

This problem is easily corrected, but requires an understanding of diabetes.

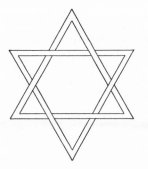

What Does "Keeping Kosher" Mean?

If you and your family have observed the laws of Kashrut for years, you probably know much more about keeping and eating kosher than you will find in this book! However, kosher food preparation may be new for some physicians, nurses and dietitians who assist patients in planning and coordinating nutritional needs with religious observances.

In this chapter, some of the basics that pertain to planning menus for individuals with diabetes will be outlined. This information is included only as a general guideline for planning and coordinating with the Diabetic Exchange Lists included in Chapter 5. For further specifics on the laws of Kashrut, please consult your orthodox rabbi.

Why do Jewish people observe the laws of Kashrut? Primarily, it is Biblically commanded. Secondarily, other explanations have been given. These include (1) health reasons, (2) to hallow the act of eating (the dining table has been compared to the altar in the Holy Temple), (3) to learn reverence for life (koshering involves removal of blood which is the symbol of life), (4) to demonstrate separation and distinctiveness (emphasizing the uniqueness of the Jewish identity) and (5) self-discipline.

Kosher vs. traif

The Hebrew word *kosher* means "proper, fit." It refers to foods that can be eaten in accordance with Jewish dietary laws, including specific categories of foods and their selection. It also refers to the slaughter, preparation and service of meat, the separation of meat and dairy products, and to the separation of cooking, serving and eating utensils.

The Hebrew word *traif*, which describes animals found non-kosher due to physical damage or imperfections, is commonly used to describe all foods that are non-kosher.

A very important aspect of planning meals according to the laws of Kashrut is the prohibition against mixing meat *(fleishig)* or poultry with dairy foods *(milchig)*. Following are some brief explanations of how these foods are appropriately used and separated.

Kosher meat

What meats can be kosher? Generally, meats which come from animals that chew their cud, have split hooves and have been slaughtered in the manner prescribed by the Torah are acceptable. Cattle, sheep, goats and deer fall into this category but pork, pork products, and rabbit are among those that are not kosher. Domesticated fowl, such as chicken, duck, geese and turkey are also acceptable.

A kosher butcher purchases meat that has been ritually slaughtered. He removes certain arteries and veins and then performs the koshering process which consists of soaking, salting and washing the meat to remove blood. Only cuts from the forequarter of the animal can be used for kosher meat products.

Cuts of kosher meat are known by different names in various places around the world. Names of some cuts as they are known in parts of the Midwestern United States follow. Diagrams indicating kosher cuts of meat are also included.

KOSHER MEAT CUTS
BEEF
Brisket
Chopped meat
Hamburger, ground chuck,
Chuck, chuck eye steak, chuck roll (pot roast, scottie)
Brust deckle
Flanken
Liver

Rib top
Short rib
Standing rib roast
Shank eye roast *(fertle off)*
Shoulder roast *(clod)*
Book roast
Rib eye
Minute steak
Rib steak
Skirt steak
London broil
Tongue

VEAL

Breast
Cutlets or chops
Clod
Book
Shoulder
Rib
Brisket
Tongue

LAMB

Neck
Shoulder chops
Shank
Rib
Breast

POULTRY

Chicken
Cornish hen
Duck
Goose
Pigeon
Turkey

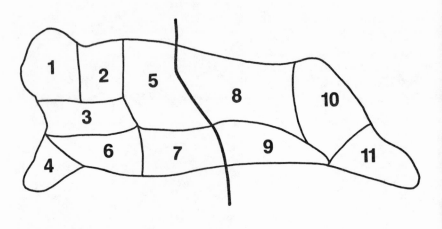

BEEF

Basic kosher cuts

1. Neck
2. Chuck
3. Shoulder
4. Foreshank
5. Rib
6. Brisket
7. Short plate

Basic non-permissible cuts

8. Loin
9. Flank
10. Rump
11. Shank

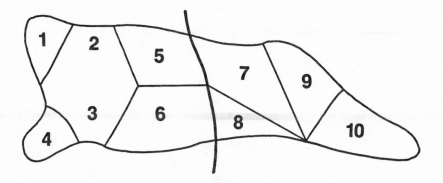

VEAL

Basic kosher cuts

1. Neck
2. Shoulder
3. Arm steak
4. Foreshank
5. Rib
6. Brisket

Basic non-permissible cuts

7. Loin
8. Flank
9. Leg
10. Hind Shank

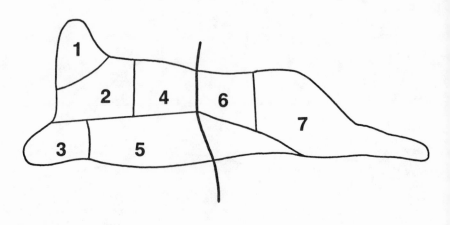

LAMB

Basic kosher cuts

1. Neck
2. Shoulder lamb chop
3. Shank
4. Rib
5. Breast brisket

Basic non-permissible cuts

6. Loin
7. Leg

Certain types of kosher meats require special procedures before they may be used. For example, liver, because it contains an excessive amount of blood, can only be koshered by broiling and should not be soaked. Meat should be koshered before it is ground for meat loaf, meat balls or hamburgers. Additionally, meat should be koshered before it is frozen for later use, unless it will be broiled.

Meats that are to be broiled need not be koshered by the soaking and salting procedure. To kosher meat by broiling, it is lightly salted on all sides. The meat is placed on a perforated rack that permits the blood to drip freely during broiling.

Several brands of frozen meat and poultry are available in supermarkets and kosher food stores. When purchasing these items, be sure to check the label to verify that the products are rabbinically endorsed.

In the processing of fowl (in the United States), a metal wing tag, called a *plumba*, bearing the symbol of the endorsing rabbinic organization, brand name and the word *kosher*, is attached to each bird. All poultry endorsed by the Ⓤ must bear such a *plumba*. Additionally, all packaged meats, sausages and poultry bearing the Ⓤ endorsement must carry the Hebrew word *kosher* as well as the Ⓤ symbol.

A word to readers on salt-free diets: Individuals on salt-free diets may feel somewhat restricted from eating meats made kosher by salting. However, soaking meat in water for two hours after koshering removes most of the salt. If you are on a salt-free diet and have questions about eating kosher meat, ask you physician.

Dairy foods and separation of foods

Dairy and meat or poultry products may not be eaten at the same meal. A meal must contain either meat or dairy products. After eating meat, it is customary to wait six hours before eating dairy products unless there is a compelling reason, such as an urgent medical problem.

After eating a dairy meal, meat foods may be eaten after rinsing the mouth and a brief wait. No period of time is Halachically required, although some few impose a restriction of one-half hour or even one hour on themselves. The exception is very hard, strong-odored cheese, such as Limburger, that necessitates a six-hour wait before eating meat.

Milk is generally kosher, although there are some intensively observant Jews who accept only *Cholov Yisroel* (milk that was taken from the cow under Jewish supervision).

All varieties of cheese require Kashrut certification, including hard cheeses such as American, Swiss, Cheddar, Muenster and soft cheeses such as such as cottage, farmer, pot and cream cheese. Cultured products and cheese products that may contain non-kosher animal rennet or stabilizers also require rabbinic certification.

Fish

Fish are considered *pareve* (neutral). Fish and meat may be eaten during the same meal but not together.

Fish must have both fins and permanent scales to be kosher. Whitefish, pike, trout, salmon, tuna and sardines are examples of kosher fish. Fish not kosher are eel, shrimp and shellfish such as oysters, crab, and lobster. Roe of non-kosher fish are also not kosher.

FISH LISTS*

To make these lists useful to the consumer, they were based on the popular names of fish. However, the popular names of fish have always been a source of error and confusion. The white perch is not a perch, for example, and very different species are sometimes given the same popular name. Nevertheless, with reasonable care, serious mistakes should not occur, and a non-kosher species should never be taken for a kosher one. The numerous cross-references will insure that none of the different kinds of fish bearing a particular name will be missed.

KOSHER FISH

Albacore See Mackerels
Alewife See Herrings
Amberjack See Jacks
Anchovies
    European anchovy
    Northern or California anchovy
Angelfish and butterfly fish
Atlantic Pomfret or Ray's bream

Ballyhoo See Flyingfish
Barracudas
Bass See Sea basses, Temperate
    basses, Sunfishes, Drums
Beluga See Sturgeons (non-kosher)
Bigeyes
Blackfish See Carps, Wrasses
Blacksmith See Damselfish

Blueback See Flounders, Herrings,
  Trouts
Bluefish or snapper blue
Bluegill See Sunfish
Blowfish See Puffers (non-kosher)
Bocaccio See Scorpionfish
Bombay duck
Bonefish
Bonito See Cobia, Mackerels
**Bowfin, freshwater dogfish, or
  grindle**
Bream See Carps, Atlantic pomfret,
  Porgies
Brill See Flounders
Buffalo fish See Suckers
Bullhead See Catfish (non-kosher)
Burbot See Codfish
Butterfish
  Pacific pompano, Harvestfish
Butterfly fish See Angelfish
Cabezon See Sculpins (non-kosher)
Cabrilla See Sea basses
Calico bass See Sunfish
Capelin See Smelts
Carps and minnows
  The carp, leather carp, mirror
  carp, Crucian carp, Goldfish,
  Tench, Splittail, Squawfish,
  Sacramento blackfish or
  hardhead, Freshwater breams,
  Roach
Carpsucker See Suckers
Caviar See Trouts and whitefish
  (salmon), lumpsuckers
  (non-kosher), Sturgeons
  (non-kosher)
Cero See Mackerels
Channel bass See Drums
Char See Trouts
Chilipepper See Scorpionfish
Chinook salmon See Trouts
Chub See Trouts, Sea chubs
Cichlids
  Tilapias, Mozambique
  mouthbrooder, Cichlids,
  Rio Grande perch
Cigarfish See Jacks

Cisco See Trouts
Coalfish See Codfish
Cobia, cabio, or black bonito
Cod, cultus, black, blue, or ling
  See Greenlings, Sablefish
Codfish
  Cod, Haddock, Pacific cod,
  Pollock, saithe, or coalfish,
  Walleye pollock, Hakes, Whiting,
  Blue whiting or poutassou,
  Burbot, lawyer, or freshwater ling,
  Tomcods or frostfish
Coho salmon See Trouts
Corbina or corvina See Drums
Cottonwick See Grunts
Crappie See Sunfish
Crevalle See Jacks
Croaker See Drums
Crucian carp See Carps
Cubbyu See Drums
Cunner See Wrasses
Dab See Flounders
Damselfish
  Blacksmith, Garibaldi
Doctorfish See Surgeonfish
Dogfish See Bowfin, Sharks
  (non-kosher)
Dolly Varden See Trouts
*Dolphin fish or mahimahis
Drums and croakers
  Seatrouts and corvinas,
  Weakfish, White seabass,
  Croakers, Silver perch, White or
  king croaker, Black croaker,
  Spotfin croaker, Yellowfin
  croaker, Drums, Red drum or
  channel bass, Freshwater drum,
  Kingfish or king whitings,
  California corbina, Spot or
  lafayette, Queenfish, Cubbyu or
  ribbon fish
Eulachon See Smelts
Flounders
  Flounders, Starry flounder,
  Summer flounder or fluke,
  Yellowtail flounder, Winter
  flounder, lemon sole, or

*Not to be confused with the *mammal* called Dolphin or Porpoise which is non-kosher

blackback, Halibuts, California halibut, Bigmouth sole, Butter or scalyfin sole, "Dover" sole "English" sole, Fantail sole, Petrale sole, Rex sole, Rock sole, Sand sole, Slender sole, Yellowfin sole, Pacific turbots, Curlfin turbot or sole, Diamond turbot, Greenland turbot or halibut, Sanddabs, Dabs, American plaice, European plaice, Brill (European turbot not included)

Fluke See Flounders

Flyingfish and halfbeaks
Ballyhoo or balao

Frostfish See Codfish

Gag See basses

Gar See Needlefish, Gars (non-kosher)

Garibaldi See Damselfish

Giant kelpfish

Gizzard shad See Herrings

Goatfish or surmullets
Kumu, Red mullet,

Gobies
Bigmouth sleeper or guavina, Sirajo goby

Goldeye and mooneye

Goldfish See Carps

Grayfish See Sharks (non-kosher)

Grayling See Trouts

Graysby See Sea basses

Greenlings
Greenlings, Kelp greenling or seatrout, Lingcod, cultus or blue cod, Atka mackerel

Grindle See Bowfin

Grouper See Basses

Grunion See Silversides

Grunts
Margate, Tomtate, Cottonwick, Sailors choice, Porkfish, Black margate, Sargo, Pigfish

Guavina See Gobies

Haddock See Codfish

Hake See Codfish

Hakes
Silver hake or whiting, Pacific hake or merluccio

Halfbeak See Flyingfish

Halfmoon See Sea chubs

Halibut See Flounders

Hamlet See Sea bass

Hardhead See Carps

Harvestfish See Butterfish

Hawkfish

Herrings
Atlantic and Pacific Herring, Thread herrings, Shads, Shad or glut herring, or blueback, Hickory shad, Alewife or river herring, Gizzard shads, Menhadens or mossbunkers, Spanish sardine, European sardine or pilchard, Pacific sardine or pilchard, Sprat

Hind See Sea bass

Hogchoker See Soles

Hogfish See Wrass

Horse mackerel See Jacks

Jack Mackerel See Jacks

Jacks and pompanos
Pompanos, palometas, and permits, Amberjacks and yellowtails, California yellowtail, Scads and cigarfish, Jack mackerel or horse mackerel, Jacks and uluas, Crevalles, Blue runner, Rainbow runner, Moonfish, Lookdown, Leatherback or lae, (Leatherjacket not included)

Jacksmelt See Silversides

Jewfish See Sea bass

John Dory

Kelpfish See Giant kelpfish

Kingfish See Drums, Mackerels

Ladyfish, or tenpounder

Lafayette See Drums

Lake Herring See Trout

Lance or launce See Sand lance

Largemouth bass See Sunfish

Lawyer See Codfish

Leatherback See Jacks
Leatherjacket See Jacks
(non-kosher)
Lingcod See Greenlings
Lizardfish
Lookdown See Jacks
Mackerel See Jacks
Mackerel, Atka See Greenlings
Mackerels and tunas
Mackerels, Spanish mackerels,
cero, and sierra, King mackerel
or kingfish, Bonitos, Wahoo,
Tunas, Skipjack tunas, Albacore
(Snake mackerels not included)
Mahimahi See Dolphin fish
Margate See Grunts
Marlin See Billfish (non-kosher)
Menhaden See Herrings
Menpachii See Squirrelfish
Merlucco See Hakes
Midshipman See Toadfish
(non-kosher)
Milkfish or awa
Mojarras
Monkeyface prickleback or eel
Mooneye See Goldeye
Moonfish See Jacks
Mossbunker See Herrings
Mouthbrooder See Cichlids
Mullet See Goatfish
Mullets
Amaamas, Uouoa, Mountain
mullets or dajaos,
Muskellunge See Pikes
Mutton hamlet See Sea bass
Muttonfish See Snappers
Needlefish or marine gars
Opaleye See Sea chubs
Paddlefish See Sturgeons
(non-kosher)
Palometa See Jacks
Parrotfish and uhus
Perch See Temperate bass, Drums,
Cichlids, Surfperches,
Scorpionfish
Perches
Yellow perch, Walleye,
pike-perch, or yellow or

blue pike, Sauger
Permit See Jacks
Pickerel See Pike
Pigfish See Grunts
Pike See Perches
Pikes
Pike, Pickerels, Muskellunge
Pike-perch See Perches
Pilchard See See Herrings
Pinfish See Porgies
Plaice See Flounders
Pollock See Codfish
Pomfret See Atlantic pomfret
Pompano See Jacks, Butterfish
Porgies and sea breams
Scup, Pinfish, Sheephead
Porkfish See Grunts
Pout See Ocean pout (non-kosher)
Poutassou See Codfish
Prickleback See Monkeyface
prickleback, Rock prickleback
(non-kosher)
Queenfish See Drums
Quillback See Suckers
Rabalo See Snooks
Ratfish See Sharks (non-kosher)
Ray See Sharks (non-kosher)
Ray's bream See Atlantic pomfret
Red snapper See Snappers
Redfish See Scorpionfish, Wrasses
Roach See Carps
Rock bass See Sunfish
Rock hind See Sea basses
Rockfish See Scorpionfish,
Temperate basses
Rosefish See Scorpionfish
Runner See Jacks
Sablefish or black cod
Sailfish See Billfishes (non-kosher)
Sailors choice See Grunts
Saithe See Codfish
Salmon See Trouts
Sand lances, launces, or eels
Sardine See Herrings
Sargo See Grunts
Sauger See Perches
Scad See Jacks
Scamp See Sea basses

Schoolmaster See Snappers
Scorpionfish
    California scorpionfish or
    sculpin, Nohus, Redfish,
    rosefish or ocean perch,
    Rockfish, Pacific ocean perch,
    Chilipepper, Bocaccio,
    Shortspine thornyhead or
    channel rockfish
Scup See Porgies
Sea bass See Temperate basses,
    Drums
Sea basses
    Black sea basses, Groupers,
    Rock hind, Speckled hind,
    Red hind, Jewfish, Spotted
    cabrilla, Gag, Scamp, Graysby,
    Mutton hamlet, Sand bass, kelp
    bass and spotted bass
Sea bream See Porgies
Sea chubs
    Bermuda chub or rudderfish,
    Opaleye, Halfmoon
Seaperch See Surfperch
Searaven See Sculpins
    (non-kosher)
Searobins
Sea-squab See Puffers
    (non-kosher)
Seatrout See Drums, Greenlings,
    Steelhead
Shad See Herrings
Sheepshead See Porgies, Wrasses
Sierra See Mackerels
Silversides
    Whitebait, spearing, or
    silversides, California grunion,
    Jacksmelt, Topsmelt
Sirajo goby See Gobies
Skates See Sharks (non-kosher)
Skipjack See Mackerels
Sleeper See Gobies
Smallmouth bass See Sunfish
Smelts
    Capelin, Eulachon
Snapper blue See Bluefish
Snappers
    Schoolmaster, Muttonfish or

    mutton snapper, Red snapper,
    Yellowtail snapper, Kalikali,
    Opakapaka, Onaga
Snooks
Sockeye salmon See Trouts
Sole See Flounders
Soles
    Sole or true sole, Lined sole,
    Hogchoker
Spadefish
Spanish mackerel See Mackerels
Spearing See Silversides
Splittail See Carps
Spoonbill cat See Sturgeons
    (non-kosher)
Spot See Drums
Sprat See Herrings
Squawfish See Carps
Squirrelfish
Steelhead See Trouts
Striped bass See Temperate
    basses
Suckers
    Buffalo fish, Quillbacks or
    carpsuckers
Sunfish
    Freshwater basses,
    Largemouth bass, Smallmouth
    bass, Bluegill, Warmouth,
    Rock bass or red eye, Crappies
    or calico basses
Surfperches
    Black perch, Pile perch, Shiner
    perch
Surgeonfish
    Tangs, Doctorfish, Unicornfish
    or kalas
Tang See Surgeonfish
Tarpon
Tautog See Wrasses
Temperate basses
    Striped bass or rockfish, Yellow
    bass, White bass, White perch,
    Giant California sea bass
Tench See Carps
Tenpounder See Ladyfish
Threadfins
    Blue bobo, Barbu

Tilapia See Cichlids
Tilefishes
    Ocean whitefish
Tomcod See Codfish
Tomtate See Grunts
Topsmelt See Silversides
Tripletail
Trouts and whitefish
    Atlantic salmon, Pacific salmon,
    Coho or silver salmon, sockeye,
    blueback or red salmon,
    chinook, king or spring
    salmon, pink or humpback
    salmon, chum, dog, or fall
    salmon, Brown trout, rainbow
    trout or steelhead, cutthroat
    trout, golden trout, Lake trout,
    brook trout, Arctic char,
    Dolly Varden, Whitefish and
    ciscos, Cisco or Lake herring,
    Chubs, Graylings
Tuna See Mackerels
Turbot See Flounders
    (some non-kosher)
Unicorn See Surgeonfish
Wahoo See Mackerel
Walleye See Perches
Walleye pollock See Codfish
Warmouth See Sunfish
Weakfish See Drums
Whitebait See Silversides
Whitefish See Trouts, Tilefish
Whiting See Codfish, Hakes,
    Drums
Wrasses
    Hogfish and aawas, Hogfish or
    capitaine, Tautog or blackfish,
    California sheephead or redfish,
    Cunner, chogset, or bergall
Yellowtail See Jacks
Yellowtail snapper See Snappers

NON-KOSHER FISH

Bullfish
    Sailfish, Marlins and spearfish
Catfish
    Channel catfish, Bullheads,
    Sea catfish
Cutlassfish
    Scabbardfish
Eels
    American and European eel,
    Conger eel
Gars, Freshwater gars
Goosefish or anglers
Lampreys
Leatherjacket
Lumpsuckers
    Lumpfish, Snailfish
Ocean pout or eelpout
Oilfish
Puffers
    blowfish, swellfish,
    sea-squab
Rock prickleback or rockeel
Sculpins
    Cabezon, Searaven
Sharks, Rays and their relatives
    Grayfish or dogfish, Soupfin
    shark, Sawfish, Skates,
    Chimaeras or ratfish
Snake mackerels
Sturgeons
    Beluga, Paddlefish or
    spoonbill cat
Swordfish
Toadfishes
    Midshipmen
Triggerfish and filefish
Trunkfish and cowfish
Wolffish or ocean catfish

These lists were prepared by James W. Atz, Ph.D., Curator and Dean Bibliographer, Department of Ichthyology, The American Museum of Natural History, New York, NY, and Adjunct Professor of Biology, Graduate School of Arts and Science, New York University.

The list is reprinted here with permission from the Union of Orthodox Jewish Congregations of America.

Pareve foods

Pareve means neutral. Fruits and vegetables are *pareve*. *Pareve* foods contain neither meat nor milk and are prepared in utensils used for *pareve* only. *Pareve* foods can be used with either a milk or meat meal. Eggs are pareve. (Eggs from kosher fowl are kosher.) However, an egg that has a blood spot in it is not considered kosher.

Breads and cereals

Many breads, cakes and cereals are kosher. Watch the ingredients carefully, however, even if the product has a kosher endorsement. These products are considered a neutral food if milk, butter or other dairy products or derivatives are not used.

If an item contains any dairy product, it cannot be used at a meat meal. Some bagels are made with dairy products and should not be classified as *pareve*. Water rolls, rye bread and pumpernickel do not have any meat derivatives; they are *pareve* and can be eaten with meat or dairy meals. Matzo, also *pareve*, is the only bread product allowed during Passover; it is also commonly used throughout the year. Whole grains such as oatmeal, barley, brown rice, *kasha* (buckweat groats) are popular. Kosher endorsement is required on bread and cereal products.

Vegetables and fruits

All vegetable and fruits may be used in a kosher diet. Some greens are very popular with certain ethnic groups. For example, spinach or sorrel leaves are used for *schav*, a popular soup. Many kosher cooks make extensive use of broccoli, carrots, sweet potatoes and yams. Green peppers are popular and are often served stuffed with meat or a dairy mixture.

Fresh and canned tomatoes are extensively used. Green cabbage is cooked slightly and may be stuffed with a ground beef and tomato sauce mixture. Root vegetables and potatoes are frequently used. *Latkes* (potato pancakes) and potato pudding prepared with eggs are very popular. Noodles or noodle pudding, as a potato substitute, is sometimes preferred to rice. Beets are often used in soups such as borscht.

Oranges and grapefruit are kosher and their juices are often used for breakfast. Grape juice or any grape product, however, must have a kosher endorsement to be considered kosher. Why? The Jewish concept of *yayin nesekh* (wine libation) applies here. This concept dates back to ancient times when wine was used for purposes of idolatry. Today, non-certified grape and wine products are still rabbinically forbidden.

Cooked or dried fruits (prunes, raisins, apples, peaches, pears, apricots) are commonly served. Fresh or stewed fruits are often eaten as desserts with the meat meal. However, dried fruits are fairly high in calories and carbohydrates and diabetics watching their calories and carbohydrates (and sugar) must be careful about snacks.

Other foods

Any product containing vegetable oils or shortening must be rabbinically certified. This includes margarine which must be labelled *pareve* to be used with meat.

Desserts made with milk are considered in the dairy products group. Ice creams and sherbets (always a dairy product) must be kosher endorsed. Any products made with non-certified animal shortening (schmaltz) are not kosher.

Soft drinks, tea, or coffee without milk are served with meat meals when milk beverages are prohibited. *Pareve* non-dairy whitener is available.

Dishes and utensils

Dishes and utensils are separated for meat and dairy meals. In homes, separate sets of these items are maintained; in some homes, separate kitchens, or separate sinks, are utilized.

In hospitals without separate facilities, disposable, single-service paper plates or pre-packaged foods are used.

Passover foods

During Passover leavened products are omitted for eight days. A leavened product contains agents that cause the product to rise. The *Torah* (Jewish law) says that the departure of the Jewish people from Egyptian slavery occurred so hastily that there was not time to prepare bread in the usual manner. As they walked to freedom, they prepared and ate *matzo* (unleavened bread).

According to the *Torah*, Jewish people should not eat or have in their possession any form of *chometz* (leavened products such as year-round bread, rolls, cakes, cookies, etc.) during the eight days of Passover. Foods made from wheat, rye, barley, oats and millet or from their derivatives can become *chometz*. Also, Ashkenazic Jews do not use rice, peas and all types of beans during Passover.

Eggs, matzo meal, and/or potato starch are common ingredients in specially prepared Passover foods. Additionally, all foods for use during Passover must be rabinnically certified and labelled as such.

In a kosher household, special dishes and utensils are reserved or specially prepared for Passover use.

There are more details about Passover foods and customs in Chapter 6.

Kosher emblems

If you are confused about kosher endorsements on prepared food products, you are not alone. There are many different symbols of kosher certification. In the United States, the nationally recognized symbol is the Ⓤ, indicating approval by the Union of Orthodox Jewish Congregations of America. (There are local endorsements, too, such as the Chicago Rabbinical Council that uses the initials cRc inside a triangle.)

Many foods do not need kosher symbols. For example, raw nuts, raw fruits and vegetables or those canned and frozen in their OWN juice (except grape) or in syrup (as in the case of fruits), certain fruit juices (orange, grapefruit, pineapple, pear, peach and apricot), rice, sugar, flour and whole unground spices do not require rabbinic certification.

The letter "D" next to a kosher symbol indicates a dairy product.

Patient education

If you are involved with patient education and must counsel a patient who has diabetes, you might want to contact your local council of orthodox rabbis for further information. Often in cases of disease or illness, patients have many questions regarding observance of the laws of Kashrut. At such times it is best to consult with a rabbi as well as the medical team and inform your patient that you have done so.

If you are a hospital dietitian planning a diet for a patient with diabetes who observes the kosher laws, you might want to talk with the hospital's Jewish chaplain (rabbi) for clarification of some of the concepts outlined in this chapter.

Now that you have some basics about the religious requirements of the kosher diet, you can assist in the planning of an appropriate and acceptable healthy diet for an individual with diabetes.

Additional sources of information are listed in Chapter 12.

Healthy Kosher Meal Planning

A healthy kosher diet includes all the basic nutrients essential for life and good health. According to the U.S. Department of Agriculture, all the necessary elements are contained within five basic food groups:

> Fruits and vegetables
>
> Breads and cereals
>
> Milk and cheese
>
> Meats, poultry, fish and beans
>
> Fats and sweets

From the fruits and vegetable group, we should have four servings each day. One should be a good source of vitamin C, such as oranges or tomatoes. Deep-yellow or dark green vegetables provide vitamin A. Unpeeled fruits and vegetables and those with edible seeds (berries) add fiber to our diet.

Four basic servings from the breads and cereals group should be included each day. Whole-grain and enriched products are preferable. Needs for basic servings of milk and cheese products differ depending on the age of the person. For example, teenagers and nursing mothers should have four servings a day while most adults only require two servings.

Two servings from the meat, poultry, fish and beans group should be included each day. Choices should be varied among these foods. Each has distinct nutritional advantages. For example, red meats are good sources of zinc. Liver and egg yolks are valuable sources of vitamin A. Dry beans and peas are good sources of magnesuim. Fish and poultry are relatively low in calories and fat. Cholesterol occurs naturally only in foods of animal origin. All meats contain cholesterol, and it is present in both the lean and the fat; the highest concentration is present in organ meats and egg yolks. Fish that is kosher is relatively low in cholesterol.

Generally, use of foods in the fats and sweets group depends on how many calories you require and what your doctor recommends. Foods like butter, margarine, mayonnaise and other salad dressings, jams, jellies, syrups, soft drinks and wine, beer and liquor are included in this group. Also included are products such as pastries and unenriched breads. Some of these foods are used as ingredients in prepared foods and some are just extras at the table. Of all the food groups, items from this group are the best to omit if you want to lose weight. Even if you do not have to lose weight, your doctor may recommend that you cut down on intake of many of these items to aid control of your diabetes.

What do calories mean?

Your doctor and dietitian will help you plan your diet to make the best use of the food you eat. During your planning sessions, you will talk about the caloric values of various foods. The calorie is a unit used to describe the energy content of food. You may equate one pound (about 454 grams) of body fat with about 3,500 calories. During the week, if you change your dining habit so that you eat 500 less calories each day, at the end of the week (all other things being equal), you will have lost one pound. Alternatively if you eat an extra 500 calories each day, over the course of a week you will gain a pound. (One large piece of apple strudel is about 500 calories.)

The U.S. Department of Agriculture advises persons who wish to lose weight to choose smaller or fewer portions of high-calorie foods and larger portions of low calorie foods. This applies to individuals with diabetes as well as others.

A good diet should give you enough calories to lose weight if you are overweight or enough calories to maintain your ideal weight. Your diet should include carbohydrates and protein, fiber, and only a little fat and sodium (salt).

COMPARISON OF CALORIE CONTENT OF COMMON FOODS*

Food Item	Amount	Calories
Apple, raw	1 medium	96
Asparagus	4 spears	12
Avocado, raw	1 average	334
Banana	1 medium	127
Beans, lima	½ cup	132
Beans, red kidney	½ cup	109
Beef, lean	4 oz.	237
Butter, regular	1 Tbsp.	102
Bread, pita, sesame	1 slice	140
Bread, pumpernickel	1 slice	79
Bread, rye	1 slice	61
Cabbage	½ cup	16
Cantaloupe	½ melon	47
Carrots	½ cup	34
Cereal, 40% bran flakes	⅔ cup	90
Cheese, American	1 oz.	116
Cheese, cottage	½ cup	117
Cheese, cream	1 oz.	99
Chicken, roasted	½ breast	99
Club soda	8 fl. oz.	0
Egg, whole	1 medium	79
Egg, yolk	1 medium	63
Egg, white	1 medium	16
Figs, raw	2 large	80
Fish		
Flounder, sole	4 oz.	90
Walleye pike	4 oz.	105
Salmon, fresh	4 oz.	246
Whitefish	4 oz.	176
Herring, fresh	4 oz.	200
Grapefruit	½ medium	41
Ice cream	1 cup	257
Lamb, lean	4 oz.	214
Lemon juice	1 Tbsp.	4
Lettuce, leaf, raw	1 cup	10
Matzo	½ (4" x 6")	70
Orange juice, fresh	6 fl. oz.	84
Potato, baked/boiled	1 medium	145
Potato chips	14 chips	161
Mayonnaise	1 Tbsp.	101

(cont. on next page)

(CALORIE CONTENT, cont.)

Milk, skim	8 fl. oz.	86
Milk, whole	8 fl. oz.	150
Orange	1 medium	47
Parsley flakes	1 Tbsp.	2
Peanut butter	1 Tbsp.	94
Prune juice	6 fl. oz.	149
Radishes, raw	5 medium	7
Raisins	1 cup	477
Rice, enriched	1 cup, cooked	186
Strawberries	½ cup	28
Sour cream	1 cup	493
Spinach	½ cup	7
Sugar, granulated	1 tsp.	15
Syrup, corn	1 Tbsp.	57
Tomato, raw	1 medium	27
Tomato juice	6 fl. oz.	36
Tea	1 cup	0
Veal, roast	4 oz.	188

* Adapted from *Composition of Foods,* Agriculture Handbook No. 8, U.S. Dept. of Agriculture, and *Nutritive Value of American Foods,* Agriculture Handbook No. 456, U.S. Dept. of Agriculture.

Note: The above calorie counts are *estimates* based on average sizes of food items used and are listed here to give you some *comparisons.*

Also, it is somewhat difficult to estimate the calorie content of some popular foods such as bagels, borscht, challah, lokshen kugel, matzo balls, potato knishes, gefilte fish, lox, corned beef, chopped liver and other favorites. Their calorie counts may vary considerably. Remember, however, that certain foods are likely to be *highly* caloric: *lekach* (honeycakes), *rugalah* (strudel) and any kind of *teiglach* (pastry).

Here are some easy-to-follow guidelines (as recommended by the U.S.D.A.) for controlling weight:

1.   Use less high-fat foods such as margarine, butter, highly marbled or fatty meats, and fried foods. Salad dressing, cream sauces, gravies, and many whipped dessert toppings are also high in fat.

2.   Cut down on soft drinks and other sweetened beverages such as ades and punches; reduce intake of pies and cakes.

3.   Cut down or eliminate alcoholic drinks.

4. Reduce portion sizes

5. Use whole milk or whole-milk products (most cheeses and ice cream) sparingly. Lowfat and skim-milk products, such as ice milk and skim-milk cheese, provide fewer calories than whole milk products.

6. Select cooking methods that help cut calories. Cook foods with little or no added fat. Trim off visible fat from meat and poultry. Either broil or roast on rack. If you braise or stew the meat, drain the meat to remove the fat. Broil or bake fish. Steam, bake or boil vegetables. Use kosher pareve vegetable cooking sprays on pans with non-stick surfaces so that greasing is not necessary.

7. Count the *noshes* (nibbles, snacks) and drinks you enjoy throughout the day.

What are carbohydrates?

Our three major energy sources from foods are carbohydrates, proteins and fats. There are differences between these sources.

Sugar and starches are the most common carbohydrates. Proteins give us energy and also contain nitrogen, an essential element for life. Fats are the most concentrated sources of calories based on weight.

Carbohydrates come in two types: simple and complex. Simple carbohydrates break down quickly and easily. Examples of sources of simple carbohydrates are table sugar, candy, and pies. The body usually releases enough insulin to clear the sugar derived from these simple carbohydrates out of the blood and move it into cells where it is used for energy. However, in a diabetic, either there is not enough insulin to do the task or the insulin is not effective and the simple carbohydrates break down and flood into the blood stream. If you have diabetes, your physician will probably recommend that you limit simple carbohydrates.

Complex carbohydrates, on the other hand, break down slowly in the intestinal tract. As a result, even with decreased insulin, blood sugar rises much more slowly after you eat these foods. Starchy foods, such as potatoes, spaghetti and bread are the best examples of complex carbohydrates.

The American Diabetes Association recommends that about half of the calories a person with diabetes eats should come from carbohydrates.

What foods contain fiber?

Dietary fiber is the part of plant food (fruits, vegetables and grains) that is not broken down by digestive juices in the intestine, as are other food elements.

Dietary fiber is important for normal functioning of the digestive tract. It "holds" water in the intestines, adds bulk to stools and softens them, and regulates the time it takes for food waste to move through the body.

Nutrition experts recommend that we select food with enough starch and fiber and that we cut down on sugar products. Among the recommended foods are whole-grain breads and cereals, some fresh fruits, vegetables and nuts. By using such foods, we obtain starch for energy and the fiber we need for good health. You can retain the fiber in the foods you eat by eating them raw or steaming them.

Researchers say that fiber can reduce after-meal blood glucose levels. Also, fiber has been found to improve ability of cells to receive and utilize insulin. In fact, in some patients with Type II (adult onset) diabetes, the need for insulin has been reduced. Some doctors say that in the future, when more research results are in, this high-fiber dietary approach to reducing insulin requirements for many with adult-onset diabetes will be even more important than it is now.

How can you tell which foods are the best sources of fiber? To give you some general ideas, the following chart gives examples of the relative amounts of fiber in servings of kosher foods.

COMPARISON OF FIBER CONTENT OF COMMON FOODS*

Food Item	Amount	Fiber (grams)
Almonds, roasted	1 cup	3.9
Apple, with peel	1 medium	2.3
Applesauce, unsweetened	1 cup	1.3
Avocado, raw, pitted	1 average	3.2
Lima beans, cooked	½ cup	1.6
Pinto beans, dry	1 cup	8.0
Beets, raw	1 cup	1.1
Blackberries, raw	1 cup	5.9
Bran	1 cup	7.8
40% bran flakes	½ cup	1.1
White bread	1 slice	0.8

Whole wheat bread	1 slice	2.1
Broccoli	½ cup	1.2
Carrots, cooked	1 cup	1.5
Cheese, American	1 oz.	0.0
Chickpeas (garbanzos)	½ cup	5.0
Corn on the cob	5" long ear	5.9
Dates, pitted	10 medium	2.3
Eggplant, cooked	1 cup	1.8
Figs, raw	2 large	1.2
Graham crackers	2½" square	1.5
Guava, raw	1 medium	5.6
Ice cream, vanilla	½ cup	0.0
Lentils	½ cup	1.2
Mango, raw	1 medium	2.7
Milk	½ cup	0.0
Orange juice	½ cup	0.0
Pear	1 medium	2.8
Peas	½ cup	1.5
Potato, baked in skin	1 large	1.2
Parsnips, cooked	½ cup	2.2
Raspberries, red, raw	1 cup	4.0
Sauerkraut, canned	1 cup	1.6
Sesame seeds, dried	1 cup	3.6
Spinach	½ cup	0.5
Squash, winter, baked	1 cup	2.6

*Adapted from *Composition of Foods,* Agriculture Handbook No. 8, U.S. Dept. of Agriculture, and *Nutritive Value of American Foods,* Agriculture Handbook No.456, U.S. Dept. of Agriculture.

Sodium in the diet

Salt goes by many names. In cookbooks we see references to table salt, kosher salt, pickling salt, coarse salt and other types of salt. All are sodium chloride, the chemical name for salt, which is about 40 percent sodium and 60 percent chloride by weight.

Sodium and chloride are both vital in our diet and both perform certain functions necessary for life. Sodium helps regulate blood pressure and the volume of blood, controls the amount of fluid around the body's cells, is essential for contraction of the heart and other muscles and for sending nerve impulses. Chloride controls water flow across cell walls, aids digestion and helps keep the blood properly chemically balanced.

Salt is the principle source of sodium in our diet. Many people say "salt" when they mean "sodium" and vice versa. You may have heard that friends or relatives are on sodium or salt restricted diets. Restriction of sodium is often part of many medically prescribed diets, especially for people with high blood pressure.

We get sodium in our daily diet from many sources. Some sodium occurs naturally in our foods. We add salt during cooking and at the table. Salt is also added by food processors. Additionally, a small amount of sodium is present in certain medicines and in drinking water.

According to the National Research Council and the U.S. Department of Agriculture, one teaspoon of salt contains about 2,000 milligrams of sodium. A "safe and adequate" sodium intake per day is about 1,100 to 3,300 milligrams for an adult. Estimates are that the average adult consumes between 2,300 to 6,900 milligrams of sodium each day.

Some foods we eat have higher sodium content than others, for example, milk, fish and meats. Fresh fruits and most vegetables, on the other hand, are relatively low in natural sodium.

To give you an idea of how much sodium is in the foods you eat, look at the following chart.

COMPARISON OF SODIUM (SALT) IN COMMON FOODS*

Food Item	Amount	Sodium (milligrams)
Apple	1 medium	2
Apple juice	6 fl. oz.	4
Beef, lean	4 oz.	74
Bread, white	1 slice	114
Butter		
regular	1 Tbsp.	116
regular, unsalted	1 Tbsp.	2
Cantaloupe	½ melon	24
Catsup, tomato	1 Tbsp.	156
Cereal		
40% bran flakes	⅔ cup	265
Cheese, cottage	½ cup	457
Cheese, Swiss	1 oz.	74
Chicken, broiled	¼ chicken	58
Coffee, brewed	1 cup	2
Corned beef	3 oz.	802
Cracker, saltine or soda	1 cracker	35

Egg, whole	1 medium	69
Fish		
Salmon, broiled	4 oz.	133
Sardines, canned, drained	3¼ oz.	598
Whitefish	4 oz.	60
Lamb, lean	4 oz.	79
Mayonnaise	1 Tbsp.	78
Milk,		
buttermilk	1 cup	257
whole	1 cup	120
Olives,		
green	2 medium	312
ripe	2 large	150
salt cured	3 medium	658
Orange juice, fresh	6 fl. oz.	4
Parsley flakes	1 Tbsp.	2
Peanut butter	1 Tbsp.	81
Pear	1 medium	1
Pickles, dill	1 average spear	232
Potato, baked or boiled	1 medium	5
Potato chips, salted	14 chips	285
Salami	1 slice	255
Salt, table	1 tsp.	2325
Sauerkraut	½ cup	777
Soy sauce	1 Tbsp.	1029
Spinach, raw	½ cup	25
Strawberries	½ cup	1
Tomato juice	6 fl. oz.	659
Tea	1 cup	1
Turkey, light meat	4 oz.	61
Worcestershire sauce	1 Tbsp.	206
Yogurt, low-fat, plain	8 oz.	159

* Adapted from *Straight Talk About Salt*, published by the Salt Institute, Alexandria, VA; *Composition of Foods*, Agriculture Handbook, No. 8, U.S. Dept. of Agriculture; and *Nutritive Value of American Foods*, Agriculture Handbook No. 456, U.S. Dept. of Agriculture.

Tips for seasoning

Instead of seasoning your food with salt, you can use herbal seasonings. Here are some tips you can follow as you prepare kosher foods appropriate for a diabetic diet:

Use fresh herbs in salads.

Use lemon juice and fresh ground pepper to enhance natural flavors.

Use orange juice as a base for meat marinade.

For poultry, use a combination of garlic, mushrooms, orange slices, dry or unsweetened kosher wine, curry, paprika, parsley, sage and onion.

For fish, use a bay leaf, dry mustard, tomato, lemon, green pepper and paprika.

For beef, use a bay leaf, marjoram, onion, fresh mushrooms, dry mustard, green pepper and ginger.

When you experiment with different spices, you'll see how delicious your foods will taste, even without salt. When you use a combination of appealing seasonings, others in the family will not feel "deprived" of salt in their food. Instead, they will be treated to a new world of flavor and eating enjoyment.

Now that you have reviewed this basic information on good nutrition and healthy ways to prepare foods, you are ready to learn about the kosher Exchange Lists system for those with diabetes.

The Exchange Lists and Your Kosher Diet

Back when your *bubbeh* (grandmother) was young, following a kosher diet appropriate for good control of diabetes was more complicated than it is now. Just the words "special diet" have always caused a little apprehension because they suggest restriction. Now, however, following a diet to control diabetes and being kosher isn't as restrictive as you might think, thanks to the Exchange Lists system developed by the American Diabetes Association and the American Dietetic Association.

The Exchange Lists can also be used for meal planning by others who must control calories and carbohydrates. The Exchange Lists as adapted for kosher use in this book can mean "waist control" for everyone.

Good nutrition plays a vital part in the management of diabetes. The kinds of foods you eat and the quantity of calories you consume each day affects your blood sugar level, whether you do or do not take insulin or oral medication. The quantity of calories you need each day is related to your weight and the amount of exercise you do. Your doctor will explain that the best way to balance your needs for calories (and insulin, if you require it) is to eat similar quantities of foods at the same time each day. Also, you will want to eat specific amounts of various types of foods so that your diet contains the proper balance of carbohydrates, proteins, fats and vitamins. The Exchange Lists that follow are your guidelines for doing this easily and effectively.

Your personal diet plan

Some diets can be very uninteresting, especially if they include structured menu plans for every day. Unlike these diets, the Exchange Lists give YOU the choice. With your dietitian's supervision and your physician's approval, you will make up your own menu plan. You can choose the foods that you like best and that are best for you. Your diet will be personally tailored for you based on the number of calories you need, your exercise habits, and whether or not you take injected insulin or oral medication to control your blood sugar level.

Because of these variables, your neighbor's diet may be a little different than yours. However, you will have enough in common with other people who have diabetes to exchange recipes and kosher menu plans. And, you will "speak the same language" in terms of calories and Exchange Lists.

Using the Exchange Lists, you will have good variety in your diet and your meals can be very much like those you prepare for others in the family (assuming you follow the general rules for good nutrition outlined in Chapter 4). However, you will want to watch your portion sizes carefully and at times dish out your serving before you add the sauces and gravies for others at the table.

Your physician will tell you how many calories you should have and the rest is up to you. But remember, you won't be alone in planning your diet, because your physician's health care team probably includes a dietitian who will help you get started in using the Exchange Lists and who will be available to answer questions that come up about every day and specific meal plans for holidays.

The Exchange Lists

The Exchange Lists are groups of measured foods of the same nutritive value that can be substituted in meal plans. There are six Exchanges, or groups:

Milk (Various types of milk and yogurt including non-fat, low-fat and whole milk).

Vegetables (Starchy vegetables are counted in the bread exchange list).

Fruit (Fruits are high in simple sugars and should be carefully measured).

Breads (Breads, cereals, and starchy vegetables such as corn, potatoes, and peas).

Meats (Divided into three sub-categories: lean meat, medium-fat, and high-fat meat). This exchange includes meats, poultry, fish, cottage cheese and certain hard cheeses rich in protein. Beans and peas are also calculated in this exchange.

Fats (Both animal fats and vegetable fats).

Foods in any one Exchange group can be substituted or traded with other foods in the same group because an exchange is a measured portion of a specific food and is approximately equal in calories and in the amount of carbohydrate, protein and fat and contains similar minerals and vitamins.

From the last chapter you remember that carbohydrates, proteins and fats are the three major energy foods. Starches and sugars are the most common carbohydrates. Proteins give us energy and contain nitrogen. Fats give us energy and are also the most concentrated source of calories. We also get calories from alcohol.

The foods on the Exchange Lists have been included to make a specific nutritional contribution to good health. No one Exchange group can supply all the needs for a well-balanced diet. Some foods from all six lists are necessary to provide all your nutritional needs.

Now, the lists. These lists are based on the "Exchange Lists for Meal Planning" by the American Diabetes Association, Inc. and The American Dietetic Association. The adaptations of these lists have been approved for medical and religious applicability by Dr. Chertack and Rabbi Berlat.

Milk exchanges

One milk exchange contains 12 grams of carbohydrate, 8 grams of protein, a trace of fat, and 80 calories. One exchange is one cup.

Milk is an excellent source of calcium, a good source of phosphorous, protein, some of the B-complex vitamins, including folacin and Vitamin B12 and Vitamins A and D. Milk can be added to coffee, tea, cereal or other foods.

MILK EXCHANGES

NONFAT FORTIFIED MILK

Skim or nonfat milk	1 cup
Powdered, nonfat dry, before adding liquid	⅓ cup
Canned, evaporated (skim)	½ cup
Buttermilk made from skim milk	1 cup
Yogurt made from skim milk (plain, unflavored)	1 cup

LOW-FAT FORTIFIED MILK

1 percent fat fortified milk (omit ½ fat exchange)	1 cup
2 percent fat fortified milk (omit 1 fat exchange)	1 cup
Yogurt made from 2 percent fortified milk (plain, unflavored) (omit 1 fat exchange)	1 cup

WHOLE MILK (omit 2 fat exchanges)

Whole milk	1 cup
Canned, evaporated whole milk	½ cup
Buttermilk made from whole milk	1 cup
Yogurt made from whole milk (plain unflavored)	1 cup

Vegetable Exchanges

One exchange of vegetables contains about 5 grams of carbohydrate, 2 grams of protein and 25 calories. One exchange is 1/2 cup.

You can enjoy your vegetables alone or in salads, soups or casseroles. You will get Vitamin A from deep yellow and dark green vegetables. Good sources of Vitamin C are asparagus, broccoli, brussels sprouts, cabbage, cauliflower, collards, kale, mustard greens and spinach, tomatoes and turnips.

VEGETABLE EXCHANGES

Asparagus	Turnip
Bean sprouts	Mushrooms
Beets	Okra
Borscht (no sugar)	Onions
Broccoli	Rhubarb
Brussels sprouts	Rutabaga
Cabbage	Sauerkraut
Carrots	Sorrel (Schav)
Cauliflower	String beans,
Celery	green or yellow
Eggplant	Summer Squash
Green pepper	Tomatoes
Greens	Tomato juice
Beets	Turnips
Chard	Vegetable juice
Kale	cocktail
Mustard	Zucchini
Spinach	

The following *raw vegetables* may be used without limitations:

Chicory	Lettuce
Chinese cabbage	Parsley
Endive	Radishes
Escarole	Watercress

Remember that the starchy vegetables are included in the Bread Exchange Lists.

Fruit Exchanges

One exchange of fruit contains 10 grams of carbohydrate and 40 calories. Citrus fruits and raspberries, strawberries, mangoes, cantaloupes, honeydews and papayas contain Vitamin C. Good sources of Vitamin A include apricots, mangoes, cantaloupes, nectarines, peaches and persimmons. Many fruits, such as bananas, oranges, apricots, nectarines and peaches are good sources of potassium.

FRUIT EXCHANGES

Apple	1 small
Apple juice	⅓ cup
Applesauce (unsweetened)	½ cup
Apricots, fresh	2 medium
Apricots, dried	4 halves
Banana	½ small
Berries	
Blackberries	½ cup
Blueberries	½ cup
Raspberries	½ cup
Strawberries	¾ cup
Cherries	10 large
Cider	⅓ cup
Dates	2
Figs, fresh	1
Figs, dried	1
Grapefruit	½
Grapefruit juice	½ cup
Grapes	12
Grape juice (Certified kosher)	¼ cup
Guava	½ medium
Kiwi fruit	1 average
Kumquat	3 medium
Lychees	⅓ cup
Mango	½ small
Melon	
Cantaloupe	¼ small
Honeydew	⅛ medium
Watermelon	1 cup
Nectarine	1 small
Orange	1 small
Orange juice	½ cup
Papaya	¾ cup
Peach	1 medium
Pear	1 small
Persimmon, native	1 medium
Pineapple	½ cup
Pineapple juice	⅓ cup
Plums	2 medium
Pomegranate	½ average
Prunes	2 medium

Prune juice	¼ cup
Raisins	2 Tbsp.
Tangerine	1 medium

Cranberries may be used without limitation if no sugar is added.

Bread Exchanges

One exchange of bread contains 15 grams of carbohydrate, 2 grams of protein, and 70 calories. One exchange is one average slice of bread or an equivalent.

Many whole-grain and enriched breads and cereals, beans and peas are good sources of iron and thiamine. Dried beans and peas are also good sources of fiber. Starchy vegetables are on this list because they contain the same amount of carbohydrates and protein as one slice of bread.

BREAD EXCHANGES

BREAD	
White (including French and Italian)	1 slice
Whole wheat	1 slice
Rye or pumpernickel	1 slice
Bialy (roll)	½
Bulke (roll)	½
Challah (1 oz.)	1 slice
Raisin	1 slice
Bagel, small	½
English muffin, small	½
Plain roll, bread	1
Frankfurter roll	½
Hamburger bun	½
Dried bread crumbs	3 Tbsp.
Pita bread	½

CEREAL

Bran flakes	½ cup
Other ready-to-eat unsweetened cereal	¾ cup
Puffed cereal (unfrosted)	1 cup
Cereal (cooked)	½ cup
Rice or barley (cooked)	½ cup
Pasta (cooked), Spaghetti, noodles, macaroni	½ cup
Popcorn (popped, no fat added)	3 cups
Cornmeal (dry)	2 Tbsp.
Flour	2½ Tbsp.
Matzo meal	2½ Tbsp.
Wheat germ	¼ cup
Kasha (Buckwheat groats) cooked	⅓ cup
raw	1½ Tbsp.

CRACKERS

Arrowroot	3
Graham, 2½" square	2
Matzo, 4" x 6"	½
Pretzels, 3⅛" x ⅛"	25
Rye wafers, 2" x 3½"	3
Saltines	6
Soda, 2½" square	4

DRIED BEANS, PEAS, LENTILS

Beans, peas, lentils (dried and cooked)	½ cup
Baked beans, (canned)	¼ cup

PREPARED FOODS

Biscuit, 2" diameter (omit 1 fat exchange)	1
Corn bread, 2" x 2" x 1" (omit 1 fat exchange)	1
Corn muffin, 2" diameter (omit 1 fat exchange)	1
Crackers, round butter type (omit 1 fat exchange)	5
Muffin, plain small (omit 1 fat exchange)	1
Potatoes, French fried, length 2" to 3½" (omit 1 fat exchange)	8
Potato or corn chips (omit 2 fat exchanges)	15
Pancake, 5" x ½" (omit 1 fat exchange)	1
Waffle, 5" x ½" (omit 1 fat exchange)	1

SPECIAL FOODS

Kichel (1" sq., no sugar)	3
Lukshen (noodles and other egg- flour mixtures, cooked)	½ cup
Potato knish (3" round)	2
Potato starch	2 Tbsp.

STARCHY VEGETABLES

Corn	⅓ cup
Corn on cob	1 small
Lima beans	½ cup
Parsnips	⅔ cup
Peas, green (canned or frozen)	½ cup
Potato, white	1 small
Potato (mashed)	½ cup
Pumpkin	¾ cup
Winter squash, acorn or butternut	½ cup
Yam or sweet potato	¼ cup

Meat Exchanges

One exchange of lean meat (1 ounce) contains 7 grams of protein, 3 grams of fat, and 55 calories. Meat is a valuable part of your diet because it is a good source of protein as well as iron, zinc and vitamins of the Vitamin B-complex. For a low-fat diet, select lean meats and trim off all visible fat.

As explained in Chapter 3, cuts of kosher meats are known by different names throughout the world. (See Chapter 3 for a list of cuts as they are known in the Midwestern United States.) Also, see Chapter 3 for diagrams of beef, lamb and veal indicating the portion of the animal from which the various cuts are taken.

Dried peas and beans, included in the Meat Exchange, are good sources of magnesium and potassium.

MEAT EXCHANGES

LEAN MEAT	
Beef	
Chuck, flank, plate	1 oz
Lamb	
Rib, shank, shoulder chops,	1 oz
Veal	
Rib, shank, shoulder, cutlets	1 oz
Poultry	
Meat without skin of chicken,	
turkey, cornish hen	1 oz
Fish	
Any fresh or frozen	1 oz
Canned salmon, tuna, in water or	
water packed	¼ cup
Sardines, drained	3
Caviar	1 oz
Gefilte fish	1 oz
Kippered herring	1 oz
Pickled herring	1 oz
Lox	1 oz
Smelts	1 oz
Cheese	
Pot cheese	¼ cup
Cheeses containing less	
than 5% butterfat	1 oz
Cottage cheese, dry and	
2 percent butterfat	¼ cup
Dried beans and peas (omit 1	
bread exchange)	½ cup

MEDIUM-FAT MEAT (for each exchange, omit ½ fat exchange)	
Beef	
Ground (15 percent fat), corned beef, rib eye, tongue	1 oz.
Liver	1 oz.
Cottage cheese, creamed	¼ cup
Cheese	
Mozzarella, ricotta	1 oz.
Farmer's cheese	or
Neufchatel	3 Tbsp.
Egg (high in cholesterol)	1
Peanut butter (omit 2 additional fat exchanges)	2 Tbsp.

HIGH-FAT MEAT (for each exchange, omit 1 fat exchange)	
Beef	
Brisket, corned beef (brisket), pastrami, ground beef (more than 20 percent fat), hamburger (commerial), chuck (ground commercial), roasts (rib), steaks	1 oz.
Chopped liver	1 oz.
Flanken	1 oz.
Lamb (breast)	1 oz.
Veal (breast)	1 oz.
Poultry	
Capon, duck (domestic), goose	1 oz.
Cheese	
American processed cheese	1 oz.
Cheddar cheese	1 oz.
Muenster cheese	1 oz.
Swiss cheese	1 oz.
Cold cuts (4½" x ⅛)	1 oz.
Frankfurter	1 small

Fat Exchanges

One Fat Exchange contains 5 grams of fat and 45 calories.

Fats come from both animals and vegetables and range from hard fats to liquid oils. Butter is an animal fat and generally remains solid at room temperature. Oils remain liquid at room temperature and are usually of vegetable origin. Commonly available kosher oils are corn oil, olive oil, peanut oil, and cottonseed oil.

Fats are a concentrated source of calories and you will want to carefully measure your intake. The following list shows the kinds and amounts of foods that contain fats to use for one fat exchange.

FAT EXCHANGES

Margarine, soft, tub, or stick*	1 tsp.
Avocado (4" diameter)**	⅛
Oil, corn, cottonseed, safflower, soy, sunflower	1 tsp.
Oil, olive**	1 tsp.
Oil, peanut**	1 tsp.
Olives**	5 small
Almonds**	10 whole
Pecans**	2 large whlole
Peanuts**	
Spanish	20 whole
Virginia	10 whole
Walnuts	6 small
Nuts, other**	6 small
Margarine, regular stick	1 tsp.
Butter	1 tsp.
Cream, light	2 Tbsp.
Cream, sour	2 Tbsp.
Cream, heavy	1 Tbsp.
Cream cheese	1 Tbsp.
French dressing***	1 Tbsp.
Italian dressing***	1 Tbsp.
Chicken schmaltz (chicken fat)	1 tsp.
Grebnes (Schmaltz cracklings)	1 tsp.
Non-dairy creams	
Powder	1 Tbsp.
Liquid	2 oz.

* Made with corn, cottonseed, safflower, soy, or sunflower oil only.
** Fat content is primarily monounsaturated.
*** If made with corn, cottonseed, safflower, soy, or sunflower oil, can be used on a fat-modified diet.

Your physician and dietitian will probably give you some Exchange Lists similar to these. You will be instructed in planning your daily meals to include foods that are good for you as well as foods you like. You will want to use available utensils, such as cups and spoons for measuring. You may also want to use a scale to weigh foods, such as meats, that have serving sizes described in ounces.

Exclusions from the Exchange Lists

Some foods have been left out of the Exchange Lists in this book because they are not necessary for a healthful diet, particularly for those who have diabetes: sugar, candy, honey, jam, jelly, cookies, syrup, condensed milk, sweetened soft drinks, pies and cake. However, you will want to talk with your dietitian and physician about including any of these foods at some times if they are appropriately prepared or appropriately sweetened. For example, you may have a pie made only with strawberries and a bran flake crust.

Unlimited foods in your diet

While there are a few restrictions in your kosher diet to control your diabetes there are also some items you can use in unlimited amounts in your meals. Your physician and dietitian will tell you more about these for your specific use, but here are some general guidelines: diet beverages (calorie free), coffee, tea, beef broth without fat, unsweetened kosher "gelatin" desserts and unsweetened pickles.

There are also many seasonings that can be used in unlimited ways to make your foods more attractive and taste appealing. You learned some tips for seasoning in the last chapter. Here are some more: lemon, lime, garlic, parsley, chili powder, paprika, celery salt, nutmeg.

Shop wisely

Watch labels when you shop for prepared foods. Be sure the labels contain the number and size of servings, the caloric content and key nutrients per serving. Remember that a label that says "dietetic" does not necessarily mean that the food is appropriate for a person who has diabetes. Also, the label does not mean that the food can be eaten in unlimited amounts. When considering a new food, even if the label says "sugar free", ask your physician and dietitian how it will fit into your personal Exchange Lists system. Also, you'll learn more about reading labels in Chapter 9.

What about favorite foods?

What should you do when faced with many mouth-watering foods not listed on your Exchange Lists at bar mitzvahs, weddings, and other parties? After you become confident about using the Exchange system, you'll develop ideas about how various foods fit into your daily meal plan and what you could eat or should avoid. Before eating any foods about which you have questions, be sure to ask your physician or dietitian. And, once you have learned to follow your Exchange Lists appropriately and have brought your diabetes under control, your doctor will advise you about just how much adjusting you can do with your daily diet plan.

Now that you have a better understanding about controlling your diabetes with appropriate diet using the Exchange Lists, you are ready for some specific recipe suggestions for good eating on holidays, Shabbat, and every day. In the next chapters you'll find some kosher recipe ideas that can be enjoyed by the individual with diabetes as well as others in the family.

Holidays, Recipes and Serving Suggestions

Much Jewish tradition centers around holidays, planning menus, preparing foods and eating. Holiday recipes and serving suggestions appropriate for those with diabetes (or those interested in controlling weight) are included in this chapter. Suggestions for Sabbath and everyday dairy and meat meals follow in Chapters 7 and 8.

This book is for readers concerned about combining good diabetes control (or weight control) with the laws of Kashrut. It is also intended for physicians, dietitians and others who may not be familiar with the Jewish holidays and the foods served at those times. For everyone, a brief synopsis of the major holidays — and the reasons for the traditional foods — is included in this chapter.

In this chapter the holidays are presented in sequence, starting with Rosh Hashanah (the New Year), and ending with Tisha B'Av (a fast day commemorating many disasters dating back to ancient times).

The Jewish New Year begins with the month of Tishrei, which approximately corresponds to September-October. (See the following calendar illustration for a better understanding of when the Jewish holidays occur throughout the year.)

CALENDAR OF JEWISH HOLIDAYS

SEPTEMBER	TISHREI	ROSH HASHANAH YOM KIPPUR SUKKOT SHEMINI ATZERET SIMCHAT TORAH
OCTOBER	CHESHVAN	
NOVEMBER	KISLEV	
DECEMBER	TEVET	CHANUKAH
JANUARY	SHEVAT	TU B'SHEVAT
FEBRUARY	ADAR	PURIM
MARCH	NISAN	
APRIL	IYAR	PASSOVER
MAY	SIVAN	YOM HA'ATZMAUT LAG B'OMER
JUNE	TAMMUZ	SHAVUOT
JULY	AV	
AUGUST	ELUL	TISHA B'AV

A style for everyone

Throughout history, Jewish people have adapted their eating habits to their circumstances. They have blended the styles of cooking of many different areas of the world with their own tastes and the laws of Kashrut.

Some Jewish cooking is based on traditional eastern European foods. That style of cooking is known as *Ashkenazic*. Examples of such foods are *knaidlach* (matzo balls), *kugel* (noodle puddings or casseroles), *gefilte* fish (chopped fish), and sweet and sour stuffed cabbage.

Another style of cooking is derived from Middle Eastern, Spanish or North African specialties and is known as *Sephardic*. Examples of such foods are stuffed eggplant, *falafel* (chick-pea-patty sandwich), and shish-ka-bob.

Jewish cooks around the world can now adapt their favorite foods to meet the needs and likes of a loved one who has diabetes (or is on a controlled diet) and learn to make new dishes that everyone can enjoy.

Measuring IS necessary

Some people never write down their own recipes. They really don't know exactly how much of each ingredient goes into each dish. If you ever asked your grandmother how to make something, you may have been told "a *bissle* (little bit) of this, and a *bissle* of that." The *bissle* system is fine for many people, but not for those on controlled diets.

Now that you are cooking for a person with diabetes, you will want to be more specific about how much of each ingredient goes into each dish and to avoid making substitutions. You will also want to know about the approximate carbohydrate, fat, protein and calorie content in each serving of each recipe. These values have been estimated for the recipes in this chapter as well as in Chapters 7 and 8.

Modifying habits

Remember that reducing the portion size of a food automatically cuts the starch, fat, and sugar in your meal. Also, you can learn to modify your traditional family recipes. You can usually reduce the sugar and oil in a recipe and still have it taste good.

Holiday entrees of chicken, turkey, veal or fish are better choices than beef or duck. They are lower in fat and calories.

NICE THINGS TO KNOW
ABOUT RECIPES IN THIS BOOK

✔ As these chapters are condensed guides to food preparation, many details relating to cooking have been omitted. Please refer to other basic cookbooks for any information not found here, such as converting decimal measurements to metric measurements, converting Fahrenheit temperatures to centigrade, or cooking in high altitudes.

✔ For details on ingredient substitutions, consult your physician or dietitian. Also, remember that use of salt substitutes requires approval by your physician.

✔ In preparing the recipes in this book, kosher corn oil was used wherever oil was specified.

✔ Vegetable pan sprays used in recipes in this book are kosher and *parevé.* When purchasing such products, check for the kosher endorsement. The vegetable spray may be helpful because it eliminates the need to grease pans and only adds negligible calories to the recipes.

✔ The diet margarine specified in this book is kosher and pareve and therefore can be used for meat and dairy dishes. Diet margarines differ in nutritional composition. Calculations in this book are based on 1 Tbsp. = 6 gms. fat, and 50 calories.

✔ When using ground meat (for example in recipes for Stuffed Cabbage and Kreplach), ask your butcher for ground meat that has no more than 15% fat content. If you don't know the fat content of the meat you are using, consider the meat in the Medium Fat Meat Exchange, not the Lean Meat Exchange. Calculations in this book for ground meat are based on very lean meat. You can decrease the fat content of the meat you use by purchasing a lean cut, trimming off all fat and grinding it yourself.

✔ Eggs used in recipes in this book are extra large unless otherwise noted. (Be sure to check your eggs for blood spots. An egg with a blood spot is not kosher.)

✔ Coarse salt is used in recipes in this book wherever salt is specified.

✔ Two types of artificial sweeteners are used. The saccharin-free sweetener mentioned is protein-derived and should be used only in recipes that do not require exposure to high temperatures. For recipes requiring cooking, that type of sweetener should be added after cooking.

How sweet is sweet?

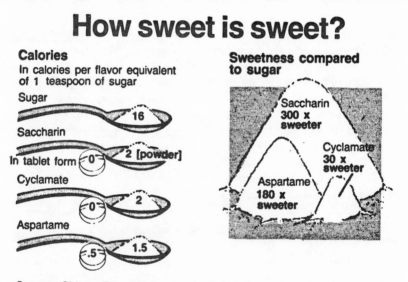

Calories
In calories per flavor equivalent of 1 teaspoon of sugar

Sugar — 16

Saccharin
In tablet form — 0 — 2 [powder]

Cyclamate — 0 — 2

Aspartame — .5 — 1.5

Sweetness compared to sugar

Saccharin 300 x sweeter

Cyclamate 30 x sweeter

Aspartame 180 x sweeter

Sources: Chicago Tribune news reports, Calorie Control Council, FDA
Reproduced courtesy of The Chicago Tribune

✔ All Exchange values and nutritional values stated in this book are *estimates*. If you are on a *very* controlled diet, please consult your physician or dietitian on how to incorporate these recipes into your daily meal plan.

✔ Remember that yields of recipes may vary slightly depending on many factors such as how finely you chop or dice ingredients or how long certain ingredients are sauteed. The estimates of Exchange equivalents stated for each recipe are based on the number of portions stated as the yield of the recipe. Remember, if you double the portion size you will also double the estimated Exchange equivalent. Similarly, you can reduce Exchange equivalents by cutting the portion size (one matzo ball in the soup instead of two).

✔ Exchange equivalents stated are based on the "Exchange Based Nutritional Analysis" (EBNA), a computer program for determining Exchange values, and the U.S. Dept. of Agriculture's Home and Garden Bulletin No. 72, "Nutrition Value of Foods". Some Exchange values have been rounded off upward to the next half.

ROSH HASHANAH

Rosh Hashanah means "head of the year" and is observed on the first two days of the month of *Tishrei*.

While Rosh Hashanah is a solemn holiday, it is also festive and festive meals are eaten in the spirit of joy and faith in God.

Traditionally, foods served in the holiday feast are heavy in starch, fat and honey. Honey is often served with a piece of *challah* (egg bread prepared in a twisted shape) or sliced apples. When dipped in honey the bread becomes a symbol of hope for sweetness and goodness during the coming year. Those with diabetes can follow the tradition by eating just a taste of the sweetness (with their physicians' permission).

The tradition of dipping bread or apple in honey may cause problems for diabetes control. Bread and fruit are quickly absorbed sources of carbohydrate and honey is a very concentrated form of sugar. A way to reduce the amount of sugar is by using a honey substitute such as an imitation maple syrup.

Traditional Rosh Hashanah, holiday, and Sabbath meals begin with wine. Dry red or white wine is a good choice for the person with diabetes. Dry Kosher wines are widely available.

Making a tzimmes

Tzimmes and honey cakes are traditional in many families. To prepare these sweet foods for persons who have diabetes, special attention must be given to the honey and sugar content.

Tzimmes can be made in many ways. Some cooks prepare it with carrots, potatoes, prunes and seasonings. Others put meat in it when the dish will be served as a main course or with a meat meal. Following is a suggestion for a way to make Tzimmes with carrots and apples that is appropriate for a person who has diabetes. (A recipe for Sweet Potato Tzimmes without meat is included in the Sukkot section.)

You will want to enjoy Tzimmes with Carrots and Apples and other recipes in this chapter as part of your Sabbath or everyday meals, too. While recipes such as this one are suggested for particular holidays, you can build your own everyday menu plans based on these recipes.

Tzimmes with Carrots and Apples

Yield: 6 small servings

Exchanges per serving: 2 Vegetable
1 Fat

INGREDIENTS
8 medium carrots (7" long), grated
1 Tbsp. uncooked barley
1 medium-sized apple, grated
3 Tbsp. pareve diet margarine
½ cup water
½ tsp. salt
2 tsp. sugar (or appropriate artificial sweetener equivalent)
⅛ tsp. ground nutmeg

PROCEDURE
1.   Combine ingredients in a 4-quart saucepan.

2.   Cover and cook over low heat for two hours or until the barley is soft. Watch it carefully and stir or add more water if necessary.

Estimated nutrients per serving
Carbohydrate: 10 gr   Protein: 4 gr
Fat: 2.5 gr   Calories: 86

(This recipe is too good to serve only on Rosh Hashanah! Once you make it you will want to prepare it for a Friday night supper or perhaps as an everyday dish.)

Rock Cornish Hen with Stuffing

Yield: 4 servings of hen, and 4 servings (½ cup each) of stuffing

Exchanges per serving: 3 Low-fat Meat
1 Bread
1 Vegetable
1 Fat

INGREDIENTS

1 Rock Cornish hen, 2 lbs. (12 oz. cooked edible meat)
Black pepper, garlic powder, paprika (to taste)
Cracker Kishke stuffing, ½ cup (see Chapter 7 for recipe)

PROCEDURE

1. Sprinkle skin of hen with spices.

2. Pack stuffing into cavity of hen. Close flap of skin over stuffing and secure shut with a skewer.

3. Place hen on rack of baking pan with its legs facing upward. Bake at 375° F for 30 minutes loosely covered with aluminum foil. Uncover and continue baking for another 60 minutes.

Estimated nutrients per serving
Carbohydrate: 7 gr   Protein: 22 gr
Fat: 9 gr   Calories: 197

You may want to serve Rock Cornish Hen with Stuffing on *erev* Yom Kippur, other holidays, or as a special main course in an everyday meal.

Rosh Hashanah Baked Apples

Yield: 4 servings

Exchanges per serving (1 large apple): 2 Fruit

INGREDIENTS

4 large baking apples (about 3½" inches in diameter*)
2 Tbsp. raisins
⅓ cup apple juice
Dash of ground cinnamon

PROCEDURE

1. Wash and core apples without penetrating the bottom of the apples. Peel a strip from the top of each apple to prevent the skin from bursting during baking. Discard the strip of skin. Arrange apples in a square baking pan.

2. Divide the raisins evenly among the 4 apples.

3. Spoon the apple juice over the apples and sprinkle the apples with cinnamon.

4. In an oven that has been preheated to 375° F, bake the apples for 40 minutes or until they look done. Baste the apples with the apple juice once after 20 minutes of baking and again before removing them from the oven.

Rosh Hashanah Baked Apples are delicious served warm or cold. They make a nice desert for an everyday meal, too.

*To make sure that the apples you have are not too small or too large for your controlled diet, place the apple, stem up, on a sheet of paper. Using a pencil, trace a circle around the outside of the apple. Measure the widest part across your circle. That is the diameter of your apple.

Estimated nutrients per serving
Carbohydrate: 15 gr   Protein: 0
Fat: 0   Calories: 60

Yom Kippur

Yom Kippur is referred to as the Sabbath of all Sabbaths. It is a 24-hour + period from sundown one day to sundown the next day devoted to prayer, fasting and atonement. It is the last day of the 10-day period of penitence beginning with Rosh Hashanah.

Yom Kippur is a holiday when physical needs are denied. The very young, the sick, those with chronic diseases (diabetes), and some pregnant women are sometimes exempt from fasting.

If you have any questions about the appropriateness of a person who has diabetes NOT fasting, please talk with your physician and/or orthodox rabbi.

While Yom Kippur is best known as a holiday during which one fasts, the *erev* Yom Kippur dinner (the evening when the holiday begins) is usually a feast. Often the symbolic foods of Rosh Hashanah are included in the *erev* Yom Kippur meal. Usually a roasted chicken, turkey or duck is served. Kreplach may float in a soup made from the fowl's giblets. Seasonal fruits may be mixed together and served with sweet wine. Dishes made with honey are often included. However, salty dishes are avoided to help prevent excessive thirst during the fast the next day.

The meal following the day-long fast is often a fairly light one.

Meat Kreplach

Yield: 12 kreplach

Exchanges per serving (2 kreplach each): 2 Lean Meat
1 Bread

INGREDIENTS
DOUGH:
1 cup unsifted flour (or ⅞ cup sifted flour)
1 egg
½ Tbsp. (or more) water
¼ tsp. salt

MEAT FILLING:
1 Tbsp. pareve diet margarine
½ lb. lean ground beef
½ cup minced onion
½ tsp. salt
¼ tsp. black pepper

PROCEDURE
1.   To prepare meat filling, heat diet margarine in a large skillet over a *low* heat, add chopped meat and onions, and cook until onions are soft, no more than 10 minutes. Stir in salt and pepper. Mixture should be completely cool before placing into dough.

2.   Prepare dough as follows: Place flour on a board, making a well in the center of the flour. Combine egg, water, and salt and pour into

the well. Work the mixture into the flour with one hand and knead until smooth and elastic. Roll out the dough and stretch it as thinly as possible.

3. Cut dough into 3" squares and place slightly more than 1 Tbsp. of filling mixture on each square. Fold over the sides to form a triangle. Press edges together with a little water and seal completely.

4. Cook filled triangles in boiling salted water or broth about 20 minutes or until they rise to the top. If cooked in water, drain and transfer to the soup.

Estimated nutrients per serving
Carbohydrate: 15 gr   Protein: 12.5 gr
Fat: 7.5 gr   Calories: 177

Sukkot

This seven-day festival begins five days after Yom Kippur. Sukkot marks the fall harvest and is highlighted with rejoicing and feasting.

Meals during Sukkot should be eaten in an outdoor booth called a *sukkah*. This is a temporary shelter used during the holiday period. The roof is covered with leaves and branches. The *sukkah* is decorated with fruits and vegetables of the harvest season such as apples, corn, pumpkin and squash.

The *sukkah* symbolizes the years when the Jewish people lived in the desert in temporary huts or dwellings after their exodus from Egyptian bondage.

Harvest foods such as stuffed peppers and stuffed cabbage leaves, squash, and sweet potatoes are traditionally served. Meat and cabbage borscht, peppery goulashes, and casseroles are part of many Sukkot celebrations. Other specialties are fruit compotes, fruit salads and tzimmes made with carrots and sweet potatoes.

Stuffed Cabbage in Tomato Sauce

Yield: 6 cabbage rolls

Exchanges per serving (1 large roll): 2 Vegetable
                                          2 Lean Meat

INGREDIENTS

6 large outer cabbage leaves
12 oz. lean ground beef or veal
½ cup cooked white rice*
1 egg**
1 tsp. dried parsley (or fresh equivalent)
¾ tsp. salt***
⅛ tsp. black pepper

Tomato sauce:
1 cup canned tomato puree
1 cup tomato juice
½ cup water
1 medium onion, diced (½ cup)
1 tsp. honey
¼ tsp. lemon juice
⅛ tsp. cinnamon

PROCEDURE

1.   Simmer cabbage leaves in a large pot in water to cover until very tender. (Be sure to select large leaves; or, use two smaller leaves for each large leaf.) Drain leaves thoroughly.

2.   In a medium-sized bowl, mix together: the meat, cooked rice, egg, parsley, salt, and pepper. Place ¼ cup of the meat mixture in the center of each cabbage leaf. Fold the sides over and roll, securing the cabbage ends with a toothpick if necessary.

3.   Combine the tomato sauce ingredients in a heavy 4- or 5-quart pot. Add cabbage rolls, seam side down, to the sauce. Spoon some sauce over each cabbage roll.

4.   Cover and simmer for 1 hour, checking occasionally to see if basting of the cabbage rolls with tomato sauce is necessary. (This recipe allows for plenty of sauce.)

5.   Serve the cabbage rolls hot.

*   Cooked brown rice may be substituted for the white rice in the meat mixture, for extra fiber. Remember, however, that brown rice

must be cooked longer than white rice. You may want to cook the rice before starting the other parts of this recipe.

**   For low cholesterol diets, use veal in place of beef and *pareve* egg substitute (if available) for egg.

***   This recipe is rather high in sodium because of the added salt in the meat mixture and the tomato products in the sauce.

Estimated nutrients per serving
Carbohydrate: 10 gr   Protein: 16 gr
Fat: 6 gr.   Calories: 158

Stuffed Acorn Squash

Yield: 4 servings

Exchanges per serving (½ squash):   1 Bread
1 Fruit
½ Fat

INGREDIENTS
2 medium acorn squash (about 4" diameter)
4 small apples (2" diameter) diced (DO NOT PEEL)
4 Tbsp. diced celery
4 tsp. minced fresh onion
4 tsp. *pareve* diet margarine, melted
4 Tbsp. water
Dash of salt
4 sprigs of fresh parsley

PROCEDURE
1.   Preheat oven to 400° F.

2.   Cut the squash in half and remove the seeds. Put the squash, cut-side down, on a baking sheet which has been sprayed with vegetable spray.

3.   Combine apples, celery, and onion in a small bowl. Add melted margarine and water. Stir. Put this mixture in a small baking dish and cover.

4.   Bake both squash and stuffing mixture for 45 minutes or until the squash is tender.

5.   Remove the squash and the apple mixture from the oven. Salt the squash, fill it with the apple mixture and insert one small fresh parsley sprig in each half.

Stuffed Acorn Squash is best eaten warm. For a quick breakfast or small lunch, use leftover stuffed squash; add sliced cheese on top, and melt the cheese under a broiler.

Estimated nutrients per serving
Carbohydrate: 25 gr   Protein: 2 gr
Fat: 2.5 gr   Calories: 131

Cabbage-Beet Borscht (Dairy)

Yield: 1 quart (4 servings)

Exchanges per 1 cup serving: 3 Vegetable
1 Fat

INGREDIENTS
½ medium onion, chopped
1 medium carrot (about 7" long), peeled and cut into
2" long thin strips
1 medium beet (3" diameter), peeled and cut into 2" long strips
1 Tbsp. oil
½ small head cabbage, cut in 2" chunks (about 4 cups
cabbage chunks)
1 small potato, peeled and cut in ½" cubes
½ of a small clove of garlic
1 bay leaf
4 oz. tomato paste
3 cups water
½ tsp. salt (or less)
⅛ tsp. black pepper
¼ cup plain skim or non-fat yogurt*

PROCEDURE

1.   Saute onion, carrot, and beet in oil in a 3-quart saucepan until the onion is tender.

2.   Add remaining ingredients except for yogurt and stir well.

3.   Bring the mixture to a boil; reduce heat. Cover and simmer for one hour or until vegetables are tender, stirring occasionally.

4.   Remove and discard garlic and bay leaf.

5.   Top each serving with 1 tablespoon of yogurt. Serve hot or warm.

*   Omit yogurt if serving Borscht with a meat meal. If the yogurt is omitted, you will reduce the calories in each servng by 20.

Note: This recipe is moderately high in sodium and may not be appropriate for persons on a strict low-sodium diet.

Estimated nutrients per serving

Carbohydrate: 15 gr   Protein: 2 gr
Fat: 5 gr   Calories: 113

Sweet Potato Tzimmes (Meatless)

Yield: 10 servings

Exchanges per serving: 1 Fruit
                                            1 Bread

INGREDIENTS

5 small sweet potatoes, peeled and cubed
3 medium carrots (7" long), peeled and grated
5.medium apples, peeled and cubed into large cubes
8 medium-sized fresh prunes (pitted)
¼ cup raisins (2 oz. or 4 tsp.)
¾ cup unsweetened orange juice
Dash of salt
Dash of ginger
1 tsp. ground cinnamon (or to taste)

PROCEDURE

1. Combine potatoes, carrots, apples, prunes and raisins in 10" skillet. Add orange juice, then spices. Stir.

2. Cook over LOW heat for about 45 minutes or until sweet potatoes are very soft.

3. Serve hot or cold.

For low-sodium diets: Reduce or omit the salt.

Estimated nutrients per serving

Carbohydrate: 25 gr   Protein: 2 gr
Fat: 0   Calories: 108

Hoshanah Rabbah

The seventh day of Sukkot is known as Hoshanah Rabbah. During a special service, the procession in the synagogue marches around the sanctuary seven times. After the service, families return home for a festive meal that usually includes kreplach. (See recipe in the Yom Kippur section earlier in this chapter.)

Shemini Atzeret and Simchat Torah

The eighth day of celebration is known as Shemini Atzeret (assembly on the eighth day). Services include prayers for rain and remembrance of the dead. In Israel this day is also celebrated as Simchat Torah.

The ninth and last day of the holiday period (in the diaspora) is called Simchat Torah (rejoicing in the Torah). It marks the end of the reading of the Torah (the first five books of the Bible). After the last lines of the Torah have been read, the opening section of the first book of the Bible is read, beginning the cycle anew.

On this joyous holiday, the Torah scroll is ceremoniously carried around the synagogue. Afterwards, fruits and sweets symbolic of the harvest sometimes are served in the synagogue. A holiday meal is then served at home.

Chanukah

Chanukah begins on the 25th day of Kislev in the Hebrew calendar and usually occurs in December. (See calendar illustration earlier in this chapter.) This is a holiday centered around fun rather than religious observance. Parties and informal get-togethers are more common than more formal family dinners.

The central theme of Chanukah is the miracle of the oil and the holiday is sometimes referred to as the "festival of lights." The lights are symbols of religious freedom.

History tells that more than 2,000 years ago, the Jewish people were dominated by Syrians who tried to force the Jews to give up their belief in God and worship other gods. The Jews were successful in forcing the foreign armies out of Jerusalem and rekindled the sacred light in the temple with pure oil.

However, while only enough oil for one day was available, it miraculously lasted for eight days. This is the reason Chanukah is celebrated for eight days.

Customarily, oil with wicks or colorful candles are lit in a menorah (candelabrum) with eight branches, one for each night of the holiday and one for a *shamash* (servant candle) which is used to light the other candles each night. On the first night, one is lit, and on each succeeding night another candle is added until eight are aglow on the eighth night. Families gather around and sing traditional songs as the candles are lit.

What about eating? This is a holiday that can be dangerous for anyone on a controlled diet! Foods fried in oil are traditional for the holiday because the miracle with which Chanukah began involved oil. *Latkes* (potato pancakes) are a popular tradition in many homes. In Israel and elsewhere, fried jelly doughnuts are favorites.

You will notice that recipes for latkes call for *frying* in oil in keeping with the miracle of the holiday. However, in the following recipe for Mini-Latkes, as little oil as possible is used and portions are fairly small to control calories.

Cauliflower tastes somewhat like potatoes but has fewer calories. The recipe for Cauliflower Latkes has fewer calories than regular latkes and also uses less oil.

Mini-Latkes (Potato Pancakes)

Yield: 8 latkes
Exchanges per serving (1 latke): 1 Bread
                                               1 Fat

INGREDIENTS

4 white potatoes (2" diameter), peeled
¼ medium onion, grated
1 Tbsp. flour
1 egg, beaten
½ tsp. salt
¼ tsp. black pepper
¼ tsp. ground nutmeg
½ Tbsp. dried chopped parsley
¼ cup vegetable oil*

PROCEDURE

1.   Coarsely grate potatoes and pat dry on paper towels. You will have about 2 cups of grated potato.

2.   To the potatoes, add the onion, flour, egg, salt, pepper, nutmeg and parsley. Mix well.

3.   Heat the oil in a large frying pan. Place 3-4 large spoonsful of the potato mixture a few inches apart on the pan. Fry until browned and crisp. Then turn and fry on the second side. Place the finished latkes in a slightly warm oven while frying the remaining latkes.

Work safely while you prepare your latkes. Place your spoonsful of the potato mixture in the pan carefully so you do not splash hot oil. Be sure to regulate the heat so that the oil does not get too hot and burn.

This recipe may be doubled to yield more servings.

4.   Serve with plain yogurt, sour cream, or sugar-free applesauce. (Please refer to Exchange Lists for values of toppings.)

*   To reduce the calorie count of each latke, use a kosher pareve vegetable spray instead of vegetable oil for frying. This reduces the calories in each latke by two-thirds. Each person can then have two or three Mini-Latkes!

Estimated nutrients per serving

Carbohydrate: 15 gr   Protein: 2 gr
Fat: 5 gr   Calories: 113

Cauliflower Latkes

Yield: 16 mini-latkes

Exchanges per serving (4 latkes): 2 Vegetable
2 Fat

INGREDIENTS

1 lb. fresh cauliflower, cut up
1 Tbsp. *pareve* diet margarine
1 small onion, chopped
3 Tbsp. unseasoned bread crumbs
1 egg, beaten
Salt and pepper to taste*
¼ cup less 2 Tbsp. oil.

PROCEDURE

1.   Remove stems and leaves from the cauliflower head. Wash it and break it into flowerets. Cook it in a large pan of boilling water, uncovered, at a high heat, for 10-15 minutes or until very tender.

2.   Heat 1 Tbsp. *pareve* diet margarine in a small frying pan. Add onion and saute over a low heat about 10 minutes or until soft and golden.

3.   Drain cauliflower thoroughly after it is cooked. Mash it with a fork until only small pieces remain.

4.   Add bread crumbs, egg, sauteed onion, and seasonings and mix well.

5.   Heat oil in a large frying pan. Take 1 Tbsp. cauliflower mixture and *kvetch* together (press together) to make it compact. Flatten into a patty about ½" thick and slide it into the pan using a spatula. Fry 8 latkes at a time.

6.   Fry until brown on each side (about 3 minutes per side). Carefully turn with a spatula. Repeat with remaining batter.

7.   Drain latkes on paper towels. Keep them warm in a 300° F oven with the door OPEN to prevent the latkes from becoming dry.

*   For low-sodium diets: Omit salt and use fresh chopped parsley instead. Use kosher unsalted diet margarine to saute the onion.

To reduce the overall fat content, fry in a pan coated with a kosher non-stick vegetable spray.

Estimated nutrients per serving

Carbohydrate: 15 gr   Protein: 9 gr
Fat: 10 gr   Calories: 186

Parslied Potato Kugel (Made with a blender)

Yield: 8 servings

Exchanges per serving: 1 Bread
1 Vegetable
1 Medium-Fat Meat

INGREDIENTS

2 Tbsp. vegetable oil
5 eggs, separated
2 medium onions, cut up
3 sprigs parsley
1 tsp. salt (or less)
¼ tsp. black pepper
5 small white potatoes, peeled and cut up
½ cup matzo meal + 2 Tbsp. (Total, 10 Tbsp.)

PROCEDURE

1.   Combine the following in this order in a blender: oil, egg yolks, onions, parsley, salt, pepper and potatoes. Blend on medium speed until the mixture is smooth.

2.   Pour the mixture into a bowl and stir in the matzo meal.

3.   Beat egg whites until they are stiff but not dry. Fold them into the potato mixture.

4.   Turn the mixture into a 9" square pan that has been "greased" with vegetable spray.

5.   Bake at 350° F for about 45 minutes or until the top is golden brown and crisp.

This is tastiest when served immediately. Parslied Potato Kugel is a nice dish to serve with any Friday evening or holiday meal.

Estimated nutrients per serving

Carbohydrate: 20 gr   Protein: 11 gr
Fat: 5 gr   Calories: 169

Tu B'Shevat

This holiday is on the 15th day of the month of *Shevat* (*Tu* means 15th). It is "New Year for Trees" and is dedicated to trees. In a desert land trees are especially important because they bear fruit, produce lumber and provide shade. Also, they and prevent soil erosion.

Foods traditionally served include many fruits such as oranges, dates, figs, a variety of nuts and carob (known as *bokser* or St. John's bread). Many people like to eat a fruit that they have not yet had during the current Jewish year.

Purim

Purim is a joyful holiday with its distinct ma'acholim (tasty foods). Friends exchange gifts of food and donate money to charity so that everyone can enjoy Purim. The exchanging of foods is referred to as *shalach manos.*

This holiday is based on a series of events in ancient Persia. An evil prime minister named Haman plotted a series of evil decrees to destroy the Jews. Mordecai, the Jewish leader and cousin to Queen Esther, learned about Haman's plan and warned the Queen, who then told her husband, King Ahasuerus. The King and Mordecai managed to interfere with Haman's plan, put Haman in a state of disgrace and Mordecai became the prime minister.

The day before Purim is a fast day because Queen Esther fasted for three days before she pleaded with King Ahasuerus to interfere with Haman's plot.

Among popular delicacies enjoyed on Purim are *hamentas-chen,* tricornered pastries which symbolize Haman's hat. The recipe for Petite Hamentaschen produces very tiny triangles appropriate for an individual on a carefully calculated diet.

Kreplach also are often served at the Purim feast because they are triangular. (See the recipe for Kreplach in the Yom Kippur section earlier in this chapter.)

For a festive main course at the Purim meal, Lemony Chicken Schnitzel is tasty and different.

Petite Hamentaschen

Yield: 30 Hamentaschen

Exchanges per serving (2 Hamentaschen): 1 Bread
1 Fruit
1 Fat

INGREDIENTS

⅓ cup margarine
2½ cups flour
3 tsp. baking powder
1 tsp. salt
¼ cup sugar
¾ cup cold water
1 egg, beaten
1 egg yolk, mixed with a little water
Flour (for "flouring" pastry board; amount varies with the baker)

Special filling:

10 teaspoons sugar-free red raspberry, pineapple, or strawberry jelly (use 3 Tbsp. + 1 tsp.)

5 tsp. orange juice concentrate (use 1 Tbsp. + 2 tsp.)

PROCEDURE

1.   Melt margarine and set aside until cool to the touch, but still liquid.

2.   Stir together flour, baking powder, and salt. Add sugar. Make a well in the center of the mixture and pour in: water, beaten egg, and cooled margarine.

3.   Beat mixture well. Then, preheat the oven to 350° F.

4.   Lightly flour a wooden pastry board and roll out a small portion of the dough as a trial. If the dough is difficult to work with, see the hints at the end of this recipe.

5.   Knead the dough several times on the floured board and roll out to a thickness of ⅛ inch. Take a small glass (about 3" diameter)

and dip it into flour. Using the floured rim of the glass as a cutter, cut out circles from the dough.

6. Place a half teaspoon of the special filling in the center of each circle. With three motions, fold the sides of the circle toward the center to form a triangle and pinch the edges tightly together. Your filling will be visible in the center of each triangle.

7. Spray cookie sheets with vegetable pan spray and arrange your triangles well apart. Brush the tops of the triangles with the thinned egg yolk.

8. Bake at 350° F for 15-20 minutes or until golden brown. Remove the Hamentaschen from the pan to a wire rack while still hot.

Estimated nutrients per serving

Carbohydrate: 25 gr   Protein: 2 gr
Fat: 5 gr   Calories: 153

Note: Petite Hamentaschen are good served warm or at room temperature. They freeze well and can be rewarmed.

Tips for working with sticky dough

(You may need these tips when making Petite Hamentaschen!) If you find out from your trial that your dough sticks too much to the pastry board, rolling pin, or your fingers, read on! Use one or all of the following tips:

1. Chill the dough first and refrigerate any portion of dough with which you are not working.

2. Lightly flour the board and the rolling pin.

3. Flour the board, set a clump of dough down, then place a sheet of waxed paper over the dough, and roll the dough with your rolling pin. Carefully peel the sheet of waxed paper off the dough and proceed to cut out the circles.

4. Remove the circle shapes from the board and place them on prepared cookie sheets. Fill and shape them into triangles on the cookie sheets as the dough will lift off easier from these than the pastry board.

Lemony Chicken Schnitzel

Yield: 4 portions

Exchanges per 3 oz. serving: 3 Lean Meat
1 Bread
2 Fat

INGREDIENTS

1 extra large egg, beaten
5 drops soy sauce
½ cup matzo meal (8 Tbsp.)
Pepper, garlic powder, dried parsley to taste
4 chicken breasts (3 oz. each; with wings and skin removed, deboned, and pounded until thin)

Sauce:

3 large mushrooms, sliced thin (½ cup)
8 tsp. pareve diet margarine
1 Tbsp. lemon juice

PROCEDURE

1.   Place egg in large soup bowl with soy sauce and stir.

2.   Combine matzo meal and spices in second soup bowl.

3.   Dip each chicken cutlet first into egg mixture, then into matzo meal mixture. Place on rack or broiler pan. Repeat for remaining cutlets.

4.   Melt margarine in a small saucepan. Add lemon juice and thinly sliced mushrooms. Let the sauce simmer until the mushrooms are tender. Remove mushrooms and set them aside.

5.   Spoon half of the sauce over the cutlets on the broiler pan. Broil for 8-10 minutes or until golden on the rack farthest from the heat source. Remove the pan from the broiler, turn the cutlets over and spoon the remaining sauce over the cutlets. Broil 2-4 minutes on this side or until golden brown.

For low-cholesterol diets: Pareve egg substitute may be used instead of egg.

For low-sodium diets: Omit the soy sauce; use unsalted pareve diet margarine.

Estimated nutrients per serving

Carbohydrate: 15 gr   Protein: 30 gr

Fat: 17 gr   Calories: 333

Passover

Pesach (Passover) is the holiday commemorating the exodus of the Jewish people from Egyptian bondage over 3,200 years ago. The first and second nights of Passover (in the diaspora) are marked with a ceremony called the *Seder* (translated this means order, or procedure). The *Seder* is a religious service conducted around the dinner table at home in which family members participate with a lavish meal served before the conclusion of the service.

The purpose of the *Seder* service is to symbolize and dramatize the important lessons of the Exodus and reemphasize the concept of freedom for all people.

The evening before the holiday begins, each homemaker makes a final search for the *chometz* (foods not kosher for Passover) remaining in the house. This is set aside and burned the next day. No leavened products are used during Passover. Special foods are prepared and special serving dishes are used during Passover.

Foods at the *Seder* table symbolize the ancient slavery and Exodus. *Matzo* (unleavened bread) is eaten to symbolize the flight of the Jews from Egypt. (There was no time to wait for the dough to rise.)

The Seder Service

The *Seder* table is the center of the Passover celebration. Upon it all the symbols of *Pesach* are gathered. A large plate is placed before the master of the household upon which are the following:

Three matzos, covered.

A roasted meatbone, as a remembrance of the time when Jewish ancestors offered a lamb sacrifice in observance of the holiday.

A roasted egg, as a remembrance of the additional festival offering by ancestors in celebration of the holiday.

Maror (bitter herbs - horseradish or romaine lettuce leaves), to remind of the bitter slavery suffered by ancient Jews during their long stay in Egypt.

Charoseth (a mixture of nuts, apples, cinnamon, and wine). This serves as a symbol of the mortar used for making the bricks with which Jewish ancestors built palaces and monuments for Pharoah.

Karpas (celery, parsley or any vegetable), which is dipped in salt water during the *Seder* service to denote the festive nature of the meal and to arouse the curiosity of the children.

A goblet of wine is placed before each person at the table. Everyone is obligated to drink four goblets of wine during the *Seder* to commemorate the redemption of the Jewish people from bondage.

In honor of the prophet, Elijah, an additional goblet of wine is placed on the table. Elijah is the symbol of peace and freedom. To symbolize the coming of Elijah, the door is opened after the meal and all rise to welcome him.

The youngest child in the family asks the traditional four questions: "Why do we eat unleavened bread? Why the bitter herbs? Why dip them in salt water? Why recline at the table?"

The father answers the questions with the historical account of the years of Jewish bondage in Egypt and the Exodus. The *Haggadah* (historic text describing Passover) is read, either by the father or alternately by all around the table.

Traditionally, each *Seder* participant drinks four cups of wine during the service. Grape juice or diluted wine may be substituted by those whose diabetes does not permit them to drink the usual amount of wine required for the holiday observance.

In many homes, the meal traditionally includes *charoseth*, chopped liver, matzo balls, fish, meat, fowls, fruit stews and special cakes. Passover Popovers add a nice touch to a *Seder* meal or weekday meal during Passover. Borscht is a favorite in many households. Tangy Kosher Grape Soda is a refreshing beverage to serve with any Passover meal.

All ingredients in the recipes suggested for Passover use that follow must be rabbinically certified kosher for Passover.

Matzo Balls

Yield: 12 small matzo balls (6 servings)

Exchanges per serving (2 matzo balls*): ½ Bread
1 Fat

INGREDIENTS

2 eggs
2 Tbsp. chicken stock, water, or sodium-free Passover club soda
1 tsp. salt
Dash of black pepper
½ cup (Kosher-for-Passover) matzo meal
2 Tbsp. diet margarine OR vegetable spread,** softened
1 tsp. dried chopped parsley (or fresh equivalent)

PROCEDURE

1. Beat eggs slightly. Add liquid and beat until frothy.

2. Fold in salt and pepper, matzo meal, margarine and parsley.

3. Cover and refrigerate for 45 minutes to 1 hour until mixture becomes firm.

4. Mix. Moisten hands and shape mixture into 12 small balls.

5. Drop into 2 quarts of boiling water; cover and cook slowly for 45 minutes.

*   To reduce the nutrients per serving, reduce each serving to one matzo ball.

**   If vegetable spread (substitute for chicken fat) is available in your area, substitute it for diet margarine to give your matzo balls a more "authentic" flavor.

Estimated nutrients per serving
Carbohydrate: 7.5 gr   Protein: 2 gr
Fat: 5 gr   Calories: 83

Passover Popovers

Yield: 12 popovers
Exchanges per popover: 1 Bread
2 Fat

INGREDIENTS

1 cup matzo meal
½ tsp. salt
2 Tbsp. sugar
1 cup water
½ cup oil
4 eggs

PROCEDURE

1.   Mix together the matzo meal, salt and sugar and set aside.

2.   Boil water and oil in a saucepan; remove from heat and carefully pour into mixing bowl.

3.   Mix matzo meal, salt and sugar into the hot liquid.

4.   Add eggs, one at a time, beating after each addition.

5.   Coat muffin tins with kosher pareve vegetable spray. Fill muffin wells about half full with batter.

6.   Bake in a pre-heated oven at 400° F for 15 minutes. Reduce heat to 375° and bake for another 45 minutes.

Note: Popover insides will be moist. If you like them drier, invert them and leave in the oven with the heat OFF and the door ajar.

Estimated nutrients per serving
Carbohydrate: 15 gr   Protein: 2 gr
Fat: 10 gr   Calories: 160
Sodium content: About equal to 1 slice of bread.

Tangy Kosher Grape Soda (A Passover beverage)

Yield: 8 cups (16 servings; each is ½ cup)
Exchanges per serving: 1 Fruit

INGREDIENTS
32-oz. unsweetened kosher grape juice
1/4 cup lemon juice
32-oz. Passover club soda (sodium-free)
Artificial sweetener to taste

PROCEDURE

1. Place ice cubes in 3-quart or larger pot.

2. Blend juices in the pot.

3. Pour the club soda down the inside of the pot slowly and stir.

4. Add artificial sweetener to taste.

5. Transfer the beverage to festive pitchers for serving on the Passover table.

For low-sodium diets: Because you have used sodium-free soda, this beverage is appropriate.

Estimated nutrients per serving
Carbohydrate: 10 gr   Protein: 0
Fat: 0   Calories: 40

Yom Ha'Atzmaut

This is Israel Independence Day, celebrated around the world by Jews. It occurs on the 5th day of the Hebrew month Iyar (April - May). Foods associated with the holiday are now traditional feasting dishes, rather than the wild plants and orange peels Israelis ate during the 1948 Siege of Jerusalem that preceded the founding of the State of Israel on May 14, 1948. Picnics and outings are popular ways of celebrating this day.

Lag B'Omer

This holiday, on the 18th day of the Hebrew month of Iyar (April - May) , recalls several events in Jewish history.

Eighteen centuries ago, Jews in the region of what was then Palestine rebelled against Roman rule to establish religious freedom and independence. A plague brought illness that killed many of the student fighters. On the 33rd day of the days between Passover and Shavuot, the plague stopped. Lag B'Omer commemorates this miracle and honors the student-soldiers. It is sometimes also known as the "scholars' holiday."

Another story is that Roman law prohibited teaching Judaism. Rabbi Simon bar Yochai was discovered teaching and fled to live in a cave with his son for 12 years. During this time, students pretending to go on picnics visited him. When the Roman Emperor Hadrian died, the rabbi and his son returned home.

This second story explains why students celebrate Lag B'Omer with picnics. Traditional holiday foods are those that can be carried in picnic baskets such as sandwiches, raw vegetables and fresh fruit.

Shavuot

Shavuot is observed seven weeks after Passover begins. Shavuot marks the giving of the *Torah* (sacred law) at Mount Sinai.

Shavuot is observed for only one day in Israel and two days in the diaspora. It has become customary in many places to serve dairy dishes using milk, sour cream or yogurt at one of the festive meals. Blintzes and cheesecakes, cheese pancakes, kreplach stuffed with cheese, sour cream cakes, or knishes are favorites in many households on Shavuot.

The tradition of eating dairy dishes on Shavuot may have originated because just after the laws of ritual slaughter were received by Moses and his people there was not enough time to prepare meat in the kosher way for the next meal. Dairy products were more convenient and a tradition began.

Fish dishes that go well with a dairy meal also are popular on Shavuot. Following are recipes for Cheese Blintzes, Herbed Fish Fillets, Zucchini Cream Soup and Strawberry Cheesecake Mousse.

Cheese Blintzes

Yield: 6 large blintzes

Exchanges per 1 blintz serving: 1½ Bread
                                             1 Medium-fat Meat

INGREDIENTS

Filling:

1 Tbsp. sugar
½ tsp. cinnamon
⅛ tsp. salt
½ tsp. vanilla extract
1 tsp. orange juice
1 egg
1 tsp. corn starch
1 Tbsp. raisins, chopped
⅔ cup dry cottage cheese (packed)

Blintz batter:

Dry ingredients:
    1 cup flour
    ¼ tsp. salt
    ½ tsp. baking powder

Wet ingredients:
    ½ cup skim milk
    ½ cup water
    1 egg
    2 Tbsp. oil

Topping: 3 tsp. diet margarine, softened

PROCEDURE

1.   Stir together *filling* ingredients in a medium-sized bowl. Refrigerate until ready to use.

2.   To prepare *batter,* sift together dry ingredients in a large bowl or a 1-quart glass measuring cup with a spout. (A dairy pitcher can be used.) Mix the wet ingredients in a small bowl and add them slowly to the dry ingredients. Stir briskly to remove lumps.

3.   Spray a large, round skillet with vegetable spray. Pour some of the thick batter to one side of the skillet. Tilt the skillet and swirl as needed to distribute the batter evenly over the bottom of the skillet. "Fry" the batter over medium heat until the edges of the crepe curl slightly and the bottom is lightly browned. Remove the blintz to a large plate.

4.   Repeat the procedure from spraying the pan to frying the blintz and removing it from the pan for each of the five remaining blintzes.

5.   Fill each blintz with about ⅓ cup filling; place the filling along the center line of each blintz, roll blintz and tuck the ends under. Place blintzes with ends tucked under, in a 9" x 13" pan which has been sprayed with non-stick vegetable spray.

6.   Bake blintzes for 15 minutes, then spread the top of each blintz with ½ teaspoon diet margarine. Then bake blintzes for about 15 minutes more or until golden.

7.   Serve with golden side up. Garnish with plain yogurt or fresh blueberries.

Estimated nutrients per serving

Carbohydrate: 23 gr   Protein: 10 gr
Fat: 5 gr   Calories: 175

Herbed Fish Fillets

Yield: 4 servings

Exchanges per 3 oz. serving: 3 Lean Meat
1 Fat

INGREDIENTS

1 lb. fish fillets, divided in 4 equal pieces. Use whitefish, cod, flounder, perch or other fish. (Cooked, fish = 12 oz.)
1 Tbsp. oil
Salt and pepper to taste
½ medium onion, sliced thin
1 medium carrot (7" long), sliced lengthwise in 2" long strips
1 Tbsp. minced fresh parsley (or equivelant of dried parsley)
½ tsp. dried basil

PROCEDURE

1. Prepare fish and preheat oven to 450° F.
2. Place each fish portion in the center of a 12" square of foil.
3. Brush each fish portion with oil. Sprinkle with salt and pepper.
4. Divide onion slices, carrot strips, parsley and basil among fish portions, and place on top of each piece of fish.
5. Close foil well. Place on shallow pan and bake 25-30 minutes. Fold back the foil and serve.

For low-sodium diets: Omit salt; a good flavor will come from the basil and parsley. Also, you may want to substitute 2 Tbsp. sour cream for the 1 Tbsp. oil.

Estimated nutrients per serving
Carbohydrate: 2 gr   Protein: 21 gr
Fat: 14 gr   Calories: 210

Zucchini Cream Soup

Yield: 6 one-half cup servings
Exchanges per ½ cup serving: 1 Vegetable
                                    ½ Skim Milk

INGREDIENTS

1 medium zucchini, grated, unpeeled*
1 small onion, chopped
½ tsp. salt
1 cup water
3 cups skim milk
Black pepper to taste
3 Tbsp. flour

*   As an alternative to zucchini, you may want to use 1 cup of broccoli. Then you will have Broccoli Cream Soup.

PROCEDURE

1. Wash zucchini but do not peel it. Grate coarsely with a hand grater or in a food processor. Chop onion into small pieces.

2. Boil the zucchini, onion and salt in the water in a covered 2-quart saucepan. Cook until the vegetables are very soft.

3. Stir in 2½ cups of the skim milk. (Reserve the remaining ½ cup for the next step.) Add salt and pepper and stir. Cook until hot but not boiling.

4. Meanwhile, prepare a smooth paste of the remaining ½ cup of skim milk and flour. Pour into the saucepan and stir constantly until the mixture boils and thickens. Garnish with parsley and serve in teacups or small bowls.

Estimated nutrients per serving

Carbohydrate: 11 gr   Protein: 6 gr
Fat: 0   Calories: 68

Strawberry "Cheesecake" Mousse

Yield: 6 servings, ½ cup each

Exchanges per serving: 2 Medium-fat Meat
2 Fruit

INGREDIENTS

½ cup evaporated skim milk, chilled

6½ packages protein-derived artificial sweetener

4 oz. Neufchatel cheese, softened

½ cup ricotta cheese (use part-skim milk ricotta when kosher brand is available), softened

1 cup diced fresh strawberries, + 6 whole fresh strawberries for garnish

½ of a 3 oz. envelope of kosher unflavored gelatin

1 Tbsp. boiling water

2½ tsp. lemon juice

1½ tsp. vanilla extract

18 tsp. graham cracker crumbs (equal to 4½ crackers, finely ground)

PROCEDURE

1. Stir together the evaporated skim milk and 1½ packages of artificial sweetener in a medium bowl. Freeze mixture for about 45 minutes or until slushy.

2. Beat cheeses, sweetener, and fresh strawberries until large pieces of strawberries disappear and mixture is smooth.

3. Stir gelatin into boiling water in a small bowl until gelatin dissolves. Add lemon juice and vanilla.

4. Add gelatin mixture slowly to slushy milk mixture and beat until stiff (about 5 minutes using an electric mixer).

5. Fold this mixture into cheese and strawberry mixture in two parts, blending well each time.

6. Sprinkle 1 tsp. graham cracker crumbs over the bottom of custard cups or other small dish, add ¼ cup "cheesecake" mixture, sprinkle 1 tsp. graham cracker crumbs over this, add another ¼ cup "cheesecake" mixture, and top with 1 tsp. graham cracker crumbs.

7. Repeat step 6 for each of the remaining 5 servings.

8. Garnish each portion with a whole fresh strawberry.

Estimated nutrients per serving

Carbohydrate: 10 gr   Protein: 11 gr
Fat: 5 gr   Calories: 123

Tisha B'Av

This holiday occurs after a nine-day period during which meat may not be eaten (except on Sabbath) and marriages may not be performed. Tisha B'Av occurs on the ninth day of the Hebrew month of Av which approximately corresponds to July-August. It is the last holiday on the Hebrew calendar.

This holiday is a fast day and commemorates many tragedies in Jewish history beginning with the destruction of the first and second temples.

Observance of the holiday begins with a simple meal before sundown, after which fasting begins and lasts until after sundown the following day. Traditional foods include hard boiled eggs dipped in ashes to symbolize mourning.

The Sabbath

Shabbat (Sabbath), begins before sunset each Friday night and ends after sunset on Saturday night. Observing the rules of Kashrut, the Sabbath, and good diabetes control allows room for cooking creatively.

The laws of Judaism do not permit cooking ON the Sabbath. This doesn't mean that only cold foods must be eaten. Foods which cook with no help from the chef and which cook continuously from the beginning of the Sabbath are permitted. That means that a slow-cooking stew can be left to cook on the stovetop in the oven, or in a slow cooking device.

A traditional Friday night dinner often includes wine, *challah* and *gefilte* fish. Horseradish is usually served with *gefilte* fish. The chicken soup with vegetables may have *lokshen* (noodles) or *knaid-lach* (matzo balls), or *kreplach*. *Kugel* (either potato or noodle casserole) may be served with roast chicken or meat. Dessert is usually fruit or pastry.

The Saturday morning lunch, or brunch, usually includes wine, *challah, gefilte* fish, egg salad or chopped liver, meat or chicken at room temperature, a hot *cholent* (stew), side dishes such as *kugel,*and dessert. The stove is NOT turned on or off during the day.

Good *balabustos* (housewives) preparing a *cholent* for a person who has diabetes will want to use meat that is less fatty and has been trimmed well. Also, a vegetarian cholent can be made without any meat, and to add moistness, a polyunsaturated oil can be used.

Whole Wheat Bread Loaf

This is a recipe for two loaves of very special bread that you may want to serve with Sabbath meals, on holidays, or wrap and send in a traditional Purim gift basket. This bread is higher in fiber than traditional white or egg challah and very tasty, too! One slice of this bread is twice as thick as most breads!

Yield: 2 loaves (9 one-inch slices per loaf)

Exchanges per serving (1 slice): 2½ Bread
1 Fat

INGREDIENTS

1 cup all-purpose flour
2½ cups whole wheat flour
2 packages dry yeast
1 Tbsp. salt (or less)
3 Tbsp. kosher vegetable shortening
2 cups water
⅓ cup honey
1 egg
2½ - 3* cups all-purpose flour

PROCEDURE

1.   Combine the first four ingredients in an electric mixer bowl.

2.   Heat shortening, water, and honey in a saucepan until warm (about 120-130° F).

3.   Add warm mixture to the flour yeast mixture.

4.   Add the egg.

5.   Beat the mixture first at a low speed for about one minute, then on medium speed for three minutes.

6.   Stir in 2½ to 3 cups of all-purpose flour so that the dough is firm.

7.   Knead for five minutes on a lightly-floured board.

8.   Place dough in a large, greased bowl and cover with waxed

paper and then a towel. Let the dough rise for one hour or until it doubles in volume.

9.   Punch down the dough with your fist.

Note: If you are using 13 or more cups of flour at one time (in making 4 loaves or additional baked goods containing flour), you will want to break off a small piece of dough, say the blessing for "Separation of bread from the dough" and burn the small piece in the oven. Consult your Rabbi or seek an explanation in a more specialized Jewish cooking manual for further information.

10.   Divide the dough into two pieces. Roll each piece into a rectangle. Starting at the narrower end, roll the dough up in "jellyroll" style. Seal by pinching the ends together.

11.   Spray two 9" x 5" loaf pans with vegetable pan spray. Place one "jellyroll" in each pan.

12.   Cover and let rise until each loaf doubles in size (about ½ hour). Preheat oven to 375° F.

13.   Bake at 375° F for 35-40 minutes.

14.   Remove loaves from pans. Cool, inverted, on a wire rack.

*   Exchange calculations are based on use of 3 cups of flour. If you use only 2½ cups, carbohydrate and calorie content will be slightly lower.

Sodium content: The sodium content of one slice of this whole wheat loaf is approximately twice as much as one slice of white bread because this slice is twice as thick as a standard slice.

Estimated nutrients per serving
Carbohydrate: 38 gr   Protein: 5 gr
Fat: 3 gr   Calories: 192

Gefilte Fish Loaf

Yield: 8 slices

Exchanges per serving: 2 Lean Meat
                                            ½ Vegetable

INGREDIENTS

¾ lb. each: skinned and boned whitefish and pike (walleye or
  Northern pike) fillets, chilled
1 medium carrot
⅓ cup cold water
1 small onion
1 egg
1¼ tsp. salt
¼ tsp. black pepper or to taste
1¼ tsp. matzo meal

PROCEDURE

1.   Grind until fine: fish fillets, carrot, cold water, and onion, in grinder, food processor, etc.

2.   Combine egg, spices, and matzo meal and add to fish mixture. Stir well.

3.   Tear piece of plastic wrap about 12" wide and place fish and egg mixture in the center. Shape fish like a rolling pin, no longer then 10". Wrap plastic wrap around the loaf, twist one end tightly and tie securely with string. Twist other end; press fish to shape and remove air bubbles. Tie second end securely.

4.   Tear a second piece of plastic wrap with the same dimensions as the first. Put fish loaf seam-side down on the plastic. Wrap fish loaf in the plastic but do not tie ends. Instead, fold ends back over the loaf.

5.   Repeat previous step, with seam of prior wrapping placed down on the next sheet of plastic wrap — four more times. Tie the ends of the last wrap securely with string. Cook immediately or refrigerate overnight on the coldest shelf.

6.   To cook: Pour 3" of water into a deep pot with a wide top. Heat the water until it simmers. Add fish package; it should float. With the cover slightly ajar, poach the fish at a slow simmer for 20 minutes. Roll the fish over and poach 20 more minutes on the second side.

7.   Carefully lift the hot fish package from the water. (You may try two large slotted spoons, one at each end, to remove the

package.) DO NOT UNWRAP. Cool to room temperature, then refrigerate the wrapped fish in yet more plastic to prevent leakage. Chill six hours in refrigerator before serving.

8. To serve, unwrap plastic layers on even more plastic wrap, aluminum foil, or a large platter to catch any fish juices. Slice and serve with horseradish.

Estimated nutrients per serving
Carbohydrate: 1 gr   Protein: 15 gr
Fat: 7 gr   Calories: 124

Chopped Liver

Yield: 6 Servings
Exchanges per 2 oz. serving: 2 Medium-fat Meat
                                  2 Fat

INGREDIENTS

12 pieces chicken liver, 1 oz. each (broiled according to the rules of Kashrut)
2 hard-cooked eggs
½ medium onion, chopped fine
Dash salt and pepper
2 Tbsp. vegetable oil

PROCEDURE

1. Put chicken livers, eggs and onions through a grinder or food processor and grind until smooth.

2. Mix in seasoning and oil and stir until well mixed.

3. For serving, place a scoop of liver on a Romaine lettuce leaf.

Estimated nutrients per serving
Carbohydrate: 0   Protein: 17 gr
Fat: 12 gr   Calories: 175

You may want to serve Chopped Liver as an appetizer with a Sabbath dinner, Sabbath lunch, or any holiday meal.

"Mock" Chopped Liver (Meatless)

Yield: 10 scoops
Exchanges per serving (1 scoop): 1 Vegetable
1 Medium-fat Meat
½ Fat

INGREDIENTS

6 medium onions, diced
4 Tbsp. pareve diet margarine, melted
4 Tbsp. chopped walnuts
6 hard-boiled eggs
1 lb.-can French-style green beans, drained
½ tsp. salt
5-10 "shakes" black pepper
Paprika for color

PROCEDURE

1.   Saute diced onions in melted margarine slowly over meduim heat, until very soft.

2.   Meanwhile, mix together the walnuts, hard-boiled eggs, and green beans, preferably in a food processor, to make a smooth paste.

Note: If mixing by hand, grind the walnuts finely. To do so, place the nuts in a large plastic bag, fasten the bag at the very end, and roll over the nuts several times with a rolling pin.

3.   Add sauteed onions to the egg mixture and process or mix until smooth.

4.   Add spices and mix well.

5.   Chill overnight. The "mock" liver usually becomes browner the next day.

6.   Scoop out the mixture. Serve atop a lettuce leaf.

For low-sodium diets: To reduce the soduim content of this recipe, use unsalted canned green beans and unsalted walnuts and reduce the amount of actual salt.

Estimated nutrients per serving
Carbohydrate: 3 gr   Protein: 8 gr
Fat: 5 gr   Calories: 69

Mock liver is nice to serve for Shabbat lunch or on any festive occasion in place of "real" chopped liver.

A word about cholent
Many cooks are unaccustomed to measuring ingredients while preparing *cholent,* a slow-cooking stew. It has always been a *bissle* or a handful of this and that. Now that you are cooking for an individual with diabetes, you will want to be more specific in your measuring of ingredients.

Following are two recipes for *cholent,* one with meat and one appropriate for a dairy meal. You may want to serve either of them for a Sabbath lunch or as a main dish with any meal.

Cholent (With Meat)

Yield: 6 main-dish servings

Exchanges per serving: 2 Lean Meat
2 Bread
1 Vegetable

INGREDIENTS
1 medium onion, cut in half
10 small white potatoes, peeled and cut in chunks
⅓ cup uncooked medium barley
½ cup uncooked lima beans (Do not presoak the beans.)
½ cup uncooked red kidney beans (Do not presoak the beans.)
18 oz.* lean shortrib (raw), cut into 2 pieces
3 Tbsp. barbeque sauce (low-calorie if available)
Water to cover all but the meat

*   Ask your butcher to weigh the raw meat for you at the time you buy it. The meat will shrink to approximately 12 ounces when the cholent is done.

PROCEDURE

1.   Place ingredients – in order – in a 4-quart slow cooker or pot. Put the meat pieces on top; pour the barbeque sauce over the meat. Add water to cover all ingredients except the meat.

2.   Cover and place the slow cooker on the source of heat one to two hours before Sabbath begins. Cook on low-medium setting until Sabbath lunchtime. Keep covered Cholent in a 250° F oven (if using an ordinary pot) from slightly prior to Shabbat until ready to serve at Shabbat lunchtime.

Estimated nutrients per serving

Carbohydrate: 35 gr   Protein: 20 gr
Fat: 6 gr   Calories: 274

Note: There is no need to use a large quantity of meat in this Cholent, because the potatoes, barley and beans provide good-quality protein.

For low-sodium diets: Replace the barbeque sauce with spices such as black pepper and garlic powder, low-sodium barbeque or other spicy sauce. If permitted, you may add salt-substitute during preparation or at the table.

Low-cholesterol diets: Persons on low-cholesterol diets are advised to use the meat-free cholent recipe which follows.

Cholent (Meatless)

Yield: 8 servings

Exchanges per serving: 1 Bread
½ Fat
1 Vegetable

INGREDIENTS

¼ cup oil (polyunsaturated)
3 medium onions, diced
¼ cup uncooked lima beans
¼ cup uncooked kidney beans

8 small potatoes, cut in chunks

½ cup uncooked barley*

½ Tbsp. salt

⅛ tsp. black pepper

⅛ tsp. garlic powder

¼ cup ketchup

3½ cups water (You may vary the amount of water in this recipe to your taste. Some like cholent soupy; others like it drier.)

3 Tbsp. soy flakes (optional) for a "meaty" taste

* If adding soy flakes, reduce the barley by the same number of tablespoons.

PROCEDURE

1. Heat oil in a heavy saucepan or slow cooker (3-4 quart size). Add diced onions and saute until soft.

2. Add beans, potatoes, barley and seasonings (and soy flakes, if desired). Add water and stir. Cover.

3. Follow step A or B.
   (A) Place the *slow cooker pot* on the heating element and set at a low speed (2-2½). Cook from 1 to 2 hours before Sabbath begins and continue cooking until lunch late Saturday morning.
   (B) Cook cholent in a *heavy saucepan* from 1 to 2 hours before Sabbath on a low flame on the top of your stove. Then place it in a 200° F oven just before Sabbath begins and leave it there until lunch late Saturday morning.

For low-sodium diets: Salt should be omitted and salt substitute can be used if desired. Salt-free ketchup should be used if available.

For low-cholesterol diets: Go ahead and enjoy! This recipe contains no cholesterol.

Estimated nutrients per serving

Carbohydrate: 20   Protein: 4 gr
Fat: 8 gr   Calories: 163

Cracker Kishke

Yield: 6 slices
Exchanges per serving (1 slice): 2 Bread
½ Fat

INGREDIENTS

4 ounces crackers (42 lightly salted, hexagonally-shaped coconut oil-sprayed crackers)
1 medium onion
1 medium carrot
1 celery stalk
¼ tsp. salt
⅛ tsp. black pepper
2 Tbsp. (1 oz.) pareve diet margarine, softened

PROCEDURE

1.   Grind crackers and vegetables together in a grinder or food processor.

2.   Add seasonings and margarine and mix thoroughly.

3.   Roll mixture in foil and seal tightly. (Kishke should resemble a long sausage.) Bake 30 minutes at 425° F or place raw inside your cholent pot and let it cook with the cholent until Sabbath lunch.

   If you want to make more kishke for future use, double the recipe, wrap the kishke in aluminum foil and put them in your freezer.
   This kishke contains NO cholesterol!

For low-sodium diets: Substitute salt-free crackers for regular crackers; substitute ¼ tsp. dried parsley or fresh equivalent for salt; use unsalted pareve diet margarine if available. Omit celery if on a *very* strict low-sodium diet.

Estimated nutrients per serving
Carbohydrate: 30 gr   Protein: 4 gr
Fat: 3 gr   Calories: 158

Egg Barley With Mushrooms & Onions

Yield: 6 servings

Exchanges per serving: 1 Bread
½ Fat

INGREDIENTS

4 qts. salted water
6 oz. uncooked egg barley
½ medium onion, chopped
6 large mushrooms, sliced thin
2 Tbsp. diet margarine
Dash of salt and pepper
Parsley sprigs

PROCEDURE

1. Boil the water, then add egg barley; boil uncovered, until tender (about 10 minutes). Pour into a colander and shake out excess water.

2. Meanwhile, simmer sliced onions and mushrooms in a small amount of water or fat-free broth in the bottom of a small frying pan until tender.

3. Add drained onions and mushrooms to the drained egg barley in the colander and mix. Add the margarine in small pieces and shake the colander until the margarine melts and is distributed evenly. Transfer to a 1½-quart casserole dish or medium-sized serving bowl.

4. Add seasonings and mix thoroughly.

5. Serve hot, garnished with parsley.

This is a nice side dish for the Sabbath dinner, any festive occasion, or an everyday meal.

Estimated nutrients per serving

Carbohydrate: 15 gr   Protein: 2 gr
Fat: 3 gr   Calories: 90

Peppery Noodle Kugel

Yield: 12 pieces

Exchanges per 2¼" x 3" serving: 1 Bread
                                     1 Fat

INGREDIENTS

8 oz. (dry) thin noodles; (makes 4 cups cooked and drained)
4 Tbsp. diet margarine, melted
2 eggs
2 Tbsp. wheat germ*
1¼ tsp. salt
⅛ - ¼ tsp. black pepper
Light dash of onion powder and garlic powder
*   Wheat germ adds fiber to this otherwise fiber-free dish

PROCEDURE

1.   Cook noodles until tender; drain in colander.

2.   Combine eggs, wheat germ, and spices together in a large mixing bowl. Add melted margarine to the noodles in the colander, then add noodles to the egg mixture and stir until well mixed.

3.   Spray a 9"-square pan with vegetable pan spray. Pour noodle mixture into the pan; using the back of a serving spoon, flatten the mixture until it is even.

4.   Bake at 375° F for 30 minutes or until lightly golden.

5.   Serve hot for Friday night dinner or at room temperature for lunch on the Sabbath.

Peppery Noodle Kugel is a light side dish to serve *erev* Yom Kippur, or with any meal throughout the year.

For low-cholesterol diets: Use eggless noodles and egg substitute.

For low-sodium diets: Note that the taste of this recipe will be altered if you do not add any salt.

Estimated nutrients per serving

Carbohydrate: 15 gr   Protein: 3 gr
Fat: 3 gr   Calories: 90

Everyday Meals

Good control of diabetes (and weight control) depends on good everyday habits of diet and exercise. Everyday meals should be well balanced and include the proper quantity of nutrients and calories as outlined in Chapter 4.

For better diabetes control (and weight control), frequent use of delicatessen-type meats, such as corned beef, pastrami and salami should be discouraged while fish and other good sources of protein should be encouraged. Cheese is another good source of protein but may not be mixed with meat meals.

Following are some additional suggestions and recipes for tasty dishes to include in everyday dairy and meat meals. You will want to refer back to the preceding pages to find additional recipes for other dishes appropriate for everyday serving.

Dairy meals

Salmonburgers and Stuffed Eggplant, Mid-Eastern Style, are two tasty dishes for serving with dairy meals.

Salmonburgers

Yield: 6 oval-shaped patties (3" x 4")

Exchanges per patty: 2 Lean Meat

INGREDIENTS

1 lb. can *pink* salmon, drained, mashed
2 eggs
Black pepper, just a dash
½ tsp. parsley flakes
⅓ cup plain low-fat yogurt
¼ cup low-fat cottage cheese
¼ medium onion, finely chopped
½ celery stalk (6-8" long), finely chopped
1 Tbsp. wheat germ flakes

PROCEDURE

1.   Mix all ingredients except wheat germ in a large bowl.

2.   Spray a 9" x 13" pan with vegetable pan spray. Form the salmon mixture into 6 oval-shaped patties about 3" x 4" and place on pan.

3.   Sprinkle the top sides of the patties lightly with the wheat germ.

4.   Bake at 350° F for 20-25 minutes. Do *not* turn patties. Remove with a spatula.

5.   Garnish each Salmonburger with a thin slice of tomato.

Note: This recipe is moderately high in sodium. It is low in cholesterol.

Estimated nutrients per serving

Carbohydrate: 1 gr   Protein: 13 gr
Fat: 6 gr   Calories: 106

Stuffed Eggplant, Mid-Eastern Style

Yield: 4 servings

Exchanges per serving (¼ eggplant): 2 Medium-fat Meat
                                         2 Vegetable
                                         ½ Fat

INGREDIENTS

One 7" long eggplant, whole, unpeeled

1 quart water

2 tsp. vegetable oil

1 medium onion, diced

1 medium tomato (2" diameter), peeled and diced

½ cup fresh sliced mushrooms

⅛ tsp. garlic powder

¾ - 1 tsp. oregano flakes

⅛ tsp. black pepper

4 oz. American cheese, grated

1 oz. Mozzarella cheese, grated

PROCEDURE

1. Boil eggplant in water for 10-15 minutes or until soft. Rotate the eggplant occasionally so all sides boil.

2. Meanwhile, heat the oil and fry the vegetables and spices until the vegetables are softened (about 10 minutes).

3. Preheat oven to 350° F.

4. Slice the eggplant in half lengthwise and remove the pulp.

5. Chop pulp and add to sauteed vegetable mixture. Cook about 20 minutes or until tender, adding a small amount of water if necessary.

6. Return mixture to the eggplant half-shells. Sprinkle with combined grated cheeses.

7. Bake at 350 ° F for 20 minutes until thoroughly heated on a large piece of aluminum foil or a cookie sheet.

8. Cut each half in two and serve immediately.

Note: This is a somewhat time-consuming recipe to prepare for an everyday meal, but you might enjoy having it as a main dish for a dairy meal once in a while.

For low-sodium diets: The only ingredients with any significant sodium content are the cheeses. When available, you may substitute salt-free cheese for one of the cheeses (preferably the 4-oz. portion of the American cheese).

For low-calorie diets: Check with your local kosher grocer to see if low-calorie American cheese is available. Using it will reduce the caloric content of this recipe.

Estimated nutrients per serving
Carbohydrate: 10 gr   Protein: 18 gr
Fat: 12 gr   Calories: 223

Meat meals

Two suggestions for everyday meat meals are Tomato-Pepper Steak and Polka Dot Rice.

Tomato-Pepper Steak

Yield: 6 small servings

Exchanges per serving: 3 Lean Meat
1 Vegetable
½ Fat

Exchanges per ½ cup cooked rice: 2 Bread

INGREDIENTS
1½ Tbsp. pareve diet margarine
2 large green peppers (4" diameter) cut in long strips
4 medium tomatoes (2½" diameter) cut in thin wedges
½ cup fresh mushrooms, sliced
1½ lbs. very lean meat strips
1 tsp. oregano flakes
Salt, pepper, and garlic powder to taste
6 oz. tomato paste.
3 cups cooked rice

PROCEDURE
1.   Saute vegetable in melted margarine in a large skillet until fork-tender. Set aside.

2. Brown the meat in the remaining margarine or in its own fat (on low heat) for about 2-3 minutes on each side. You may want to put the meat in a single layer and brown half the meat at a time.

3. Return the vegetables to the skillet. Add the spices and tomato sauce. Stir. Cover and cook on a low heat until the meat and vegetables are tender.

4. Serve hot over rice.

For low-sodium diets: Omit the salt and use salt-free tomato paste.

Estimated nutrients per serving

Carbohydrate: 7 gr   Protein: 31 gr
Fat: 14 gr   Calories: 271

Polka Dot Rice

Yield: 4 servings

Exchanges per serving: 1 Bread
                                  ½ Fat

INGREDIENTS

½ cup uncooked rice (1½ cups, cooked)
⅛ tsp. lemon juice
½ cup + 1 Tbsp. frozen peas
Non-protein sugar substitute (to taste)
½ medium onion, diced (purple onion adds a nice color)
1 Tbsp. oil.
4 sprigs fresh parsley for garnish

PROCEDURE

1. Cook rice in water as directed on the package and add the lemon juice.

2. Cook the peas. Add the sugar substitute to the peas. (Use non-protein artificial sweetener only.)

3. Saute the onion in oil until golden.

4. Add peas and onion to the rice. Garnish with parsley.

Estimated nutrients per serving
Carbohydrate: 15 gr   Protein: 2 gr
Fat: 2 gr   Calories: 91

Eat and enjoy!

Now you have many new ideas for holidays, Shabbat and everyday meals. You can use the suggestions in these chapters as guides to help you plan meals for your family. Enjoy trying the recipes. You will find that most are fairly easy to prepare and are tasty and enjoyable to eat. The person who has diabetes need not have a different diet at all. Just a "calculated" diet.'

If you are on a tightly controlled diet, you may want to ask your physician or dietitian about some of the dishes and their ingredients. Remember, figures stated for nutrient values and Exchanges per serving are *estimates*.

What about other special days? Special days can be good or not so good. For example, traveling is a special circumstance, particularly for one who has diabetes. And, of course, sick days are special in another way. For details on these and other occasions, read on.

Kosher "Convenience" Foods

If you have diabetes or the person for whom you prepare meals has diabetes, you can enjoy the convenience of commercially prepared kosher foods.

Many kosher food processors and manufacturers around the world prepare conveniently packaged foods in cans, jars, boxes, and frozen forms. Each year, additional manufacturers bring out additional kosher products. There are hundreds of companies producing these products and the list of prepared foods grows longer each year.

How can you determine if commercially prepared kosher foods are appropriate for your diet? A few manufacturers provide data on nutritional information, such as percentage of fat, protein and carbohydrate in each product and amount of calories and sodium per serving. However, for most food products, you must learn how to rely on the labels on the packages. Additionally, before using commercially prepared products or serving them to someone who has diabetes, you may want to discuss the products with your physician or dietitian.

Reading labels on kosher food products

Nutrition labeling is a valuable tool to help the individual who has diabetes understand how to use products, recognize the amount and kind of carbohydrate, protein, fat and calories in packaged products,and provide more variety in the diet.

In the Winter, 1983 issue of *The Diabetes Educator,* publication of the Diabetes Education Association, an excellent article on reading labels appeared; an adapted version of the article follows. It provides good, concise answers to some of the concerns about reading labels.

To make the best use of information included on labels, the one who cooks for a person with diabetes must understand what information on the label means.

The label will provide the following information:

- Ingredients are listed in descending order of predominance by weight. The first ingredient is the largest proportion of total ingredients (or about 70% average).

- "Dietetic" foods will state how many calories of carbohydrate, fat, protein or sorbitol are present in a serving of a certain size. (But remember, the word "dietetic" doesn't necessarily mean that the item is appropriate for your controlled diet.)

- "No sugar added" on the label means that no sucrose (cane or beet sugar) has been added, but other simple sugars in the form of fruit juice or fructose or dextrose may be present.

- "Sugar free" means that the product contains little or no sugar in either natural or added form and that it is also reduced in calories. (Again, the "Sugar free" label doesn't mean unlimited use for persons on a controlled diet.)

- "Nutritive sweetener" identifies a sweetener containing calories. Examples of nutritive sweeteners are: invert sugar, corn syrup, corn sugar, dextrin, sorghum, molasses, honey, maple, or brown sugar.

- "Non-nutritive sweetener" indicates that the sweetener does not contain calories.

- Any chemical term ending in -ose usually means a form of sugar, e.g., sucrose, fructose, maltose, lactose,* levulose, glucose (or dextrose). If some form of sugar is listed in the first three ingredients of the product, the product should be used sparingly or avoided. Cellulose cannot be digested by humans, so it is not a source of sugar.

- Starch, flour, milk powder, glycerol and dextrin are all forms of carbohydrate that raise your blood sugar level.

*a dairy product

- Breakfast cereals that have more than three grams of sucrose are not recommended for use in a diabetic meal plan.

- Salt is often a hidden ingredient; diabetics who have been told to watch their salt intake should use the ingredient listing as a clue to the salt content in the product. When the label includes salt, sodium citrate, sodium hydroxide, monosodium glutamate, sodium propionate or sodium nitrate, the product should be used sparingly or avoided.

- The type of fat in the product is also of concern, especially if the fats are saturated. Coconut oil, palm oil, and cocoa butter are examples of saturated fats. (So are butter and schmaltz or chicken fat.) Partially hydrogenated or hardened oils have more saturated fat than unsaturated fat.

Avoid foods with no labels regarding nutritional information. However, some manufacturers will provide nutritional information if you write for it.

Interpreting labels

It may take some practice and motivation to interpret product information and adjust it to your individual diet plan. Following are some principles you can use to practice calculations:

1. Use a simple, basic product label. Identify the serving size and ingredients without looking at the nutrient analysis.

2. From the label, estimate the amount of ingredients in that serving size basing figures on the largest amount, which is listed first, to the smallest amount.

3. Use the Exchange Lists to identify the carbohydrate, protein, fat and calories for the serving size which is listed on the label.

4. Total the figures.

5. Compare the figures with the known values on the label.

Alternatively, you may use another procedure to convert product information to food exchanges:

1. Convert the grams of carbohydrate into bread, fruit, or vegetable exchanges.

2. Convert the grams of protein into meat exchanges, remembering

first to deduct the grams of protein in the bread and vegetable exchanges.

3. Convert the grams of fat into fat exchanges, remembering again to first deduct the fat contained in the meat exchanges.

Example: Condensed Cream of Mushroom Soup

Nutrition information per 1/2 can condensed portion (makes one 10 fluid ounce serving) —

Portions per container: 2

Prepared with water

Calories 150

Protein .... 2 grams

Carbohydrate (CHO) .... 13 grams

1 serving = 1 bread exchange (15 grams CHO, 2 grams protein)
        2 fat exchanges (10 grams fat)

How to know if convenience foods are kosher

Around the world, various emblems are used to denote "kosher." There are too many to list here. However, the leading kosher certification in the United States is the Kashrut program of the Union of Orthodox Jewish Congregations of America, operated in conjunction with the Rabbinical Council of America as its Halachic authority.

The certification mark of this body is the Ⓤ. The Ⓤ is the largest national, non-profit, public service program for kosher certification, covering more than 10,000 products. Through its supervision of key raw materials and ingredients, it acts as the foundation of the kosher food industry throughout the world, making Ⓤ certified products obtainable in communities where kosher food had previously been unavailable. The Ⓤ emblem assures the manufacturer and the consumer that the products and services bearing Ⓤ endorsement are under contractual agreement and rabbinically supervised.

A complete listing of commercially prepared foods that have been certified kosher by the Union of Orthodox Jewish Congregations of America is available. It may be of interest to consumers at home, hospital dietitians or physicians wishing to advise patients regarding special diets. There is a charge for the directory. You may obtain information regarding the current cost by writing to:

Union of Orthodox Jewish Congregations of America
45 West 35th Street
New York, New York 10018

Their "Kosher Directory" is a list of Ⓤ certified kosher products for the current year, excluding products covered by private label agreement. The products listed in the directory are divided into three categories: Dairy, Meat and Pareve. What do these classifications mean to you as a shopper and menu planner?

Dairy: These items are listed under a DAIRY designation. Items so designated are products which contain dairy ingredients as well as products which do not contain milk ingredients but which have been prepared on dairy equipment.

Meat: These items are listed under MEAT or POULTRY designation.

Pareve: Unless otherwise indicated, the listed item is *pareve*. Such items contain no dairy or meat ingredients and have been processed on *pareve* equipment. They may be eaten with either meat or milk.

All whole frozen kosher poultry must have the Ⓤ metal seal on the wing. The liver must be removed from the cavity and broiled separately. When purchasing Ⓤ packaged meat or poultry parts, be sure that both the sealed package and the inner cellophane wrapper have not been tampered with. The word *Kosher* must appear on the label.

If the Ⓤ products you want are not available where you shop, ask your grocer to stock them for you.

Updates on new products that have been certified kosher appear quarterly in the News Reporter section of the Orthodox Union publication, *Jewish Action.* Passover products under Ⓤ supervision are published annually in the Passover Products Directory.

Where to write

Various rabbinical councils in the United States and elsewhere publish directories of products they certify. Three such councils are in Chicago, Detroit and Baltimore.

Chicago Rabbinical Council
3525 West Peterson Avenue
Chicago, Illinois 60659

Vaad Horabonim of Greater Detroit
17071 West Ten Mile Road
Southfield, Michigan 48075

Vaad Hakashrus
Dept. KN
7504 Seven Mile Lane
Baltimore, Maryland 21208

Enjoy variety!

With the availability of so many kosher "convenience" foods, your controlled diet can be as varied as that of other members of your family. Learn more about your Exchange Lists system. Plan your meals wisely. Shop carefully and ask your physician or dietitian when you have questions about using certain products of combinations of foods in a meal or a day. Enjoy variety in your diet while you control your diabetes and your weight.

Traveling, Sick Days, and Special Care

Jewish holidays are special days. Additionally, for individuals who have diabetes, there are other days when special considerations have to be given to diet, exercise and medication. Some of those times are when traveling, when eating out, when not feeling well at home and when in a hospital. At all times, special attention must be given to certain aspects of personal care.

Time changes

If your travel plans call for going to an area with a time change of two hours or more, talk with your health care team about possible changes in your daily meal plan, schedule for insulin injections or oral medication. You will probably be advised to stick to your "home time" for injections and meals. This may take some prior arranging with airlines, trains or ships. Also, you can carry some of your own food to assure yourself of having it when you need it. You may be advised to change your daily food intake plan if you must sit for long periods of time without any exercise.

Kosher meals as you travel

Those who observe the laws of Kashrut can make special arrangements regarding meals while traveling. For example, kosher meals can be ordered on airlines, trains and ships. Tell your travel agent about your special needs at the time you make your reservations.

If you are traveling on El Al, the Israeli national airline, you do not have to specify that you want a kosher meal on your flight. El Al maintains its own fully equipped kosher kitchens. Passengers on airlines other than El Al should be sure that their kosher food boxes are sealed with an official certification label. Passengers requiring kosher food on any Sunday flight should order it by Friday.

Kosher meals served en route are usually meals that have been prepared in a kosher kitchen and frozen. Because they are reheated in non-kosher ovens, the meals must be reheated in exactly the way they are packaged, that is, totally wrapped in double foil with the caterer's seal and the Rabbinic certification seal intact. By the intact seal, you will know that the meal has not been tampered with. However, remember that the kosher certification only applies to the food in the sealed package. Any other food, such as snacks, wines, cheese, and coffee creamers served loose by the carrier are not included in the Kosher endorsement.

Kosher meals on flights in the United States usually are accompanied by a card from the caterer who prepared the meal. Typical of the messages which the kosher diner may find on his/her meal tray is the following:

> "This Glatt Kosher Meal is prepared under the supervision of the Union of Orthodox Jewish Congregations of America.
>
> All dishes, silver and trays used for the Kosher Meal on this flight have never been used before.
>
> Due to the nature of Kosher Meal preparation, we are unable to provide green salad. We extend to you a hearty appetite and a pleasant journey."

If you have diabetes and plan to order a meal from a transportation carrier ahead of time, inquire about the content of the meal. A typical meal for an individual with diabetes might consist of a chicken breast with lemon sauce, noodles, carrots, a soft roll and a piece of fresh fruit.

Contact your dietitian regarding the calories, carbohydrates and fats in the meal you will have aboard an airplane so that you can calculate your daily meal plan around it. After you become a seasoned diabetic traveller, you may be able to do the calculations yourself.

Ask your physician how closely you must stick to your prescribed meal plan while you travel. Some people with well-controlled diabetes have more leeway in terms of what they eat than others, and for them, traveling kosher is easier than for individuals whose disease is not so well-controlled.

Eating out

Restaurant meals, meals served at hotels and resorts, and catered meals should not be considered kosher unless they are supervised by a reputable Rabbinic authority. Some people assume that vegetarian restaurants are kosher. This is not so because fish, baked goods, cheese, shortening, oil, eggs, margarine, dressings and condiments are among the many food items requiring supervision for maintaining Kashrut. Reputable Kashrut supervision is the best guarantee that the food being served is kosher.

Most major cities with large Jewish populations have kosher restaurants. If you are planning to travel and eat in restaurants, you might find *The Jewish Travel Guide* helpful. This useful book lists kosher restaurants around the world as well as places of specific interest to Jewish visitors. You can obtain a copy of this paperback directory at your local bookstore.

Dining with the *mispocheh* (family)

What about eating at homes of relatives and friends? When invited, let your hosts or hostesses know that you are on a controlled diet. Be ready to give some suggestions for what you can and cannot eat. Eat small portions. Just taste some dishes. (If your diabetes is under good control, your physician may tell you if it is alright for you to alter your menu plan slightly once in a while.) Drink artificially sweetened beverages.

Packing tips

Some individuals who have diabetes must carry supplies of insulin and other anti-diabetes medications with them. Specially insulated kits for carrying such items are available, but are not always necessary. A more essential item is a letter of prescription for an insulin syringe and needle in case your materials are lost while traveling.

Persons with diabetes should always carry snacks as recommended by their physician and dietitian. If self-monitoring has been recommended for home care, the monitoring equipment should be carried and used while traveling.

In case of diabetic emergencies while traveling in the United States, one can contact the local affiliate of the American Diabetes Association for assistance. In other countries, similar organizations provide help. *(See chapter 12.)*

The *Kinder* (children)

Although this book has been largely concerned with the care and feeding of adults who have diabetes, in some families, the *kinder* (children), too, have diabetes. There are special summer camps for children with diabetes which feature programs to teach them how to care for themselves. Such camps also provide healthful recreative activities. The American Diabetes Association and the Juvenile Diabetes Association can provide details on these camps.

If your child with diabetes goes to a regular summer camp featuring kosher food, you should advise the camp director and dietitian about the child's dietary requirements.

Information about a diabetic child's condition should be given to school officials, too. The teacher should know if between meal snacks are part of the child's daily menu plan and if the child must test urine or blood sugar levels before lunchtime. School personnel should know how to reach the child's physician, parents or caretakers at all times.

What about a little *Shabbat* wine?

Can a person who has diabetes have a little alcoholic drink now and then? The answer to this question really must come from your physician who is familiar with your individual needs regarding your diabetes as well as your overall health. Ask for advice about the timing of your drinking and find out what types of alcohol you can safely drink. For a person with *well-controlled* diabetes, an occasional well-timed drink can be calculated into the daily menu plan with no harmful effects.

Sick days

Every day isn't perfect. Colds, flu and upset stomachs bother everyone at some time. If you have diabetes, these problems may present some special concerns. If your appetite isn't up to par, or if you cannot keep food or liquid down, you may want to call your physician. Sometimes you will be advised to make adjustments in your schedule of insulin or oral medication to allow for your change in eating habits. If you have been advised to self-monitor your glucose level, doing so will be especially important on days when you are not feeling well.

Hospital stays

Most individuals who have diabetes never have to be hospitalized. If their disease is well controlled, they can take care of themselves at home. However, there are times when some individuals with diabetes must be hospitalized.

Many hospitals in the United States and throughout the world have kosher food service. Kosher food service can be provided through various means. In many institutions, the entire kitchen operation is kosher and kosher food is served to all patients and employees of the hospital. In other institutions, a small, separate kosher kitchen is maintained to provide kosher meals for those who request them. Additionally, because of the many commercially prepared frozen foods, kosher meals usually can be provided whenever requested.

Your physician will discuss your individual dietary needs with the hospital dietitian. When you leave the hospital, you will receive a new menu plan to follow at home.

In a hospital without a kosher kitchen, kosher food is served to the hospital patient on paper dishes or disposable plastic or aluminum containers along with disposable eating utensils as is usually done on airlines serving kosher trays.

In addition to the care of diabetes, there are a few things hospital dietitians should know about patients who follow the laws of Kashrut. For example, some Jewish people observe certain restrictions on the Sabbath (sunset Friday to sunset Saturday) including such activities as writing and tearing things. They may not fill out the next day's menu on Saturday. Also, they may request that someone tear open their frozen meals for them.

Also, patients may request a bottle of unopened kosher wine or one that they have brought from home for ceremonial purposes. They may request additional food for the Friday evening meal.

They may want meat or chicken for both the Friday evening and the Saturday lunch.

Dietitians in hospitals treat each menu order individually. Each individual who has diabetes is unique and consultations with physicians and patients are essential. Following the dietary laws while in the hospital, even if critically ill, is very important to patients who maintain kosher diets.

Yom Kippur and illness

Abstention from all food and drink is required on Yom Kippur. *(See chapter 6.)* Pregnant women and nursing mothers must observe the fast. Women within three days after childbirth are excused, as is any patient whose life may be endangered by fasting.

When fasting cannot be permitted, the amount of food and drink given to the patient should be reduced to the minimum compatible with safety. According to the Chicago Rabbinical Council, it is preferable to consume small quantities (for example, one tablespoon of cereal, 3/4 ounce of juice, milk or other liquid) at nine minute intervals rather than to eat or drink a larger amount within a shorter period. In all cases of questions regarding illness and fasting, consult your physician and a member of the Orthodox Rabbinate.

Getting personal

Special care of skin, feet, eyes and teeth is particularly important if you have diabetes. This is because diabetes can cause changes in the tiny blood vessels that carry nutrients throughout your body and make you especially vulnerable to certain infections and disorders.

Skin disorders such as dry itchy skin, bacterial and fungal infections can occur more easily in weakened skin. Following a few simple guidelines can avoid many possible problems. For example, after bathing, use talcum powder in the skin folds in the armpits, the groin and under the breasts to help yourself stay dry. Avoid excessively hot water when bathing. Use a moisturizer on your skin when the humidity is low. Use a humidifier at home to moisturize your skin during cold months. Take care of injuries to your hands and feet right away.

After bathing, dry your feet thoroughly. Trim your toenails carefully and avoid cutting into the corners. Be careful about going barefoot at home and at swimming pools and beaches. Be sure your shoes and socks fit well and do not cause corns and calluses. Avoid getting blisters on your feet.

Your physician will look into your eyes during routine examinations. This is because the tiny blood vessels in the eyes may show effects of diabetes and may give some clues about changes in your condition. Damage to vision is a fairly common side effect of diabetes. That is one of the many good reasons for "tight" control of your diabetes.

To protect your precious eyesight, have your eyes checked regularly by an ophthalmologist. Have your ophthalmologist and your diabetologist confer with each other. Don't rub your eyes unnecessarily.

Wear sunglasses when outdoors in bright sunlight or on snowy days. Wear protective eyewear while doing active sports activities and while using any kind of machinery that may cause flying particles. Use adequate lighting when reading and working. Avoid eye fatigue.

Be sure that your dental care team knows that you have diabetes. They may wish to contact your physician before any procedures are performed. Brush your teeth regularly and carry a pocket or purse-sized brush so that you can brush your teeth when away from home. Avoid using too-hard toothbrushes that might irritate the delicate tissues of your mouth.

Personal care for the individual who has diabetes really involves no more than ordinary good health care habits. However, for the diabetic, special attention to good habits can mean the difference between unwanted complications and good control of the disease.

Ess Gesundterheit

Although you now know more about following your controlled kosher diet specially planned for you by your physician and your dietitian, you may still have many questions about your diabetes and your overall good health. What causes diabetes? What can you do to be healthier? How can you keep track of your own condition? What may be in the future for those with diabetes?

Why me?

Experts still don't know a lot about the causes of diabetes. They know, however, that certain factors may lead to the development of diabetes. One factor is heredity. You may have a tendency to develop diabetes if other members of your family had it. However, even if your parents did not have diabetes, you can have it. Sometimes diabetes skips generations.

In people with a family history of diabetes (as well as those without), certain stresses may encourage development of the disease. Being a little too *zoftig* (overweight) is such a stress because it affects the body's utilization of insulin. About 80 percent of all the people with diabetes are overweight at the time they are diagnosed as having diabetes.

So, if you have a history of diabetes in your family, lose a little weight. Even if you don't have the family history but are overweight, if your doctor advises you to lose weight, follow the advice!

Other stresses affect the development of diabetes, too. Stress can be psychological or physical. Surgery, serious infections, accidents, and taking medications are all considered "stresses."

Pregnancy also gives the body extra stress. Sometimes diabetes is diagnosed in women who have had repeated miscarriages. And, sometimes diabetes is diagnosed in pregnant women. When this happens, it may or may not be a temporary situation. However, if you become pregnant and know that you have diabetes, tell your obstetrician right away so that special precautions will be taken to assure a safe delivery of a healthy infant.

Minimize your risk of other diseases

Your healthy diet to control your diabetes can also have other good effects. One benefit is a reduction of your risk of developing cardiovascular disease. Many people who have diabetes (especially Type II as described in Chapter 2) also have high blood pressure because there are some common factors in both diseases.

Diabetes, high blood pressure, obesity, lack of exercise, emotional stress, high cholesterol levels and cigarette smoking are all risk factors for coronary artery problems and other diseases of the circulatory system.

If you have diabetes you can minimize the other risk factors of coronary artery disease by cutting down on the amount of fat and salt you eat. Too much salt in the diet has been kown to affect blood pressure in some individuals. Hypertension, or high blood pressure, puts extra strain on the heart and blood vessels and can also aggravate atherosclerosis, a condition marked by hardened and clogged arteries.

Some researchers say that fat and cholesterol consumption influences atherosclerosis and that people whose cholesterol levels are high are more likely to develop clogged and hardened arteries than those with lower levels. Saturated fats are derived from animal products and are usually solid at room temperature. Examples are butter and chicken fat. Fats obtained from vegetable products are known as "unsaturated" fats and they are usually liquid at room temperature. Unsaturated fats are considered more healthful than saturated fats, say the experts.

Stay active!

Being active is good for you because exercise can help you control your weight. Exercise also makes insulin work more effectively to reduce your blood glucose level. Exercise can also make your heart and lungs work more efficiently and contribute to a reduction of high blood pressure and relief of physical tension. Exercise may also reduce cholesterol levels in your blood; this may happen because exercise increases the amout of certain proteins called "high-density lipoproteins" (HDLs) which remove cholesterol from the blood.

Exercise doesn't mean that you have to start jogging or lifting weights if you haven't done those things before. Just more ordinary walking may be enough for you. You may be advised to use stairs instead of elevators wherever possible. You may be advised to join a community organization that makes a swimming pool available. Or, you may enjoy participating in a group that does mild calisthenics.

Each individual has different needs for exercise and different interests. Ask your physician what is best for you. Your weight, the type of diabetes you have, and whether or not you are insulin-dependent will influence your individually tailored exercise plan.

Keep an eye on your doctor!

It has been said that 50 percent of the time, prescription medications are improperly taken.* One reason for the failure to follow instructions is that patients do not ask enough questions when they are given a prescription.

To be sure that you understand your doctor's instructions regarding a new medication, be sure to ask your doctor these questions:

- What is the name of the drug?
- What is it supposed to do for me?
- How and when do I take it? (For example, before meals, after meals, etc.)
- When should I stop taking it?
- What food, drinks, other drugs or activities should I avoid while taking the drug?
- What possible side effects might occur?

*FDA Consumer, July-August, 1983

• Is there any written information available about the drug?

If you go to any physician in addition to your diabetologist, be sure to say that you use insulin or oral medication (if you do). Ask how the new medication, if one is prescribed for you, will interact with what you are already taking.

Keep an eye on yourself (or the one you love)

Your physician will want to see you at regular intervals. In between visits, you may be advised to watch your own glucose levels by techniques known as self-monitoring. It may be important for you to have a day-by-day reading or readings several times a day. Such readings will permit you to adjust the amount of insulin you take if you are insulin-dependent, or to adjust the quantity of food you eat or the amount of exercise you do.

Control of diabetes is a delicate balance of diet, exercise, insulin, and your emotional health. Careful self-monitoring is especially important for those individuals who have what is known as "brittle" diabetes. This term means that wide swings in blood sugar levels occur. Also, self-monitoring is important for individuals who have complications of diabetes such as eye or kidney problems.

Monitoring blood glucose levels at home is especially important for women who have diabetes who plan to conceive, those who are pregnant, diabetics with frequent hypoglycemia and diabetics who have difficulty achieving adequate control of their disease.

Your physician will help you become familiar with various methods of self-testing that you can do at home or while traveling. Your physician will advise you about the appropriateness of using blood or urine self-tests for your individual condition.

Blood or urine specimens are used in the self-tests. One type of test involves using a drop of blood and specially treated strips of paper which are then compared for color changes. Some people who have poor vision may do better with a specially designed digital readout device instead of comparing strips by appearance alone.

Some urine tests involve placing a few drops of urine in a test tube, adding water and a specially prepared tablet which reacts to the glucose in the urine. A comparison of the color of the test tube liquid is made with a color chart. Another type of urine test involves dipping a tiny strip or stick into the urine, waiting a few seconds for a reaction and then comparing color changes.

What's ahead?

No cures for diabetes are available at this time. However, better ways of controlling diabetes are being developed each year. For example, animal research has led many scientists to believe that the day may not be far off when a small portion of a healthy pancreas may be transplanted into an individual with diabetes as a means of controlling the diabetes.

From this research, small portable insulin pumps have been developed. Researchers are now looking at the advantages of tiny implantable insulin pumps which are controlled by computer and release just the right amount of insulin at the appropriate time based on the individual's needs.

There are advantages and disadvantages of such pumps. They permit a continuous infusion of insulin all day long and throughout the night with extra doses of insulin before meals, permitting the body to use its sugar more normally at all times. However, a needle must be implanted in the wearer's skin. Also, the user must remember to set dials several times a day, such as before meals.

In terms of prevention of diabetes, researchers are also working on means of identifying possible viruses which may trigger the start of diabetes. While this research may not help you now, it may be of value to future generations.

Is diabetes a "Jewish" disease?

Although the question has been considered earlier in this book, there is more to be said on the matter. There is a "rabbinic style" answer to the question. On the one hand, maybe yes, and on the other hand, maybe no.

Although some physicians say they believe that the incidence of diabetes among Jewish people seems to be higher than in other groups, this belief has never been scientifically validated. Richard M. Goodman, M.D., commented on the incidence of diabetes in Jews in his book, *Jewish Genetic Diseases*[1]. He quoted a statement made by Fishberg in 1911[2]. "The testimony of many physicians who have had a large experience with diabetes mellitus goes to show that it occurs from two to six times as frequently in Jews as it does among the people around them." However, Goodman pointed out that Fishberg concluded by saying: "On the whole, there is no justification for considering diabetes a disease of Jews. It has not been observed to be more frequent among the Jews in every country than among their non-Jewish neighbors." Goodman also said that in 1928 Sir Humphrey Rolleston[3] repeated the "twice to six times as high" statement and added that the records of the Metropolitan Life Assurance Company of New York supported this impression. Goodman further stated another opinion, that of Sorsby and Sorsby[4], who in 1932 wrote: "Most clinicians hold that diabetes mellitus is undoubtedly more frequent among Jews, though a negative view is held by good authorities."

Goodman pointed out that surveys of diabetes conducted in Israel do not indicate extremely high rates of this disease among Jews. He said: "Whether or not this holds true for Jews in the Diaspora as well can be shown only through surveys outside Israel. Most studies have not been designed to answer the specific question of whether or not diabetes is more common among Jews than among non-Jews. Therefore, current comparative information from other studies is at best speculative."

Is diabetes a "Jewish" disease? Maybe and maybe not. It will take more definitive scientific data than exists at this time to answer the question.

Incidence of diabetes does differ, however, between countries or areas. Tables 1 and 2 give some worldwide information.

1.   Goodman, Richard M., M.D., *Genetic Disorders Among the Jewish People,* The Johns Hopkins University Press, Baltimore and London, 1979.

2.   Fishberg, M., *The Jews: A study of Race and Environment,* Charles Scribner's, New York, 1911

3.   Rolleston, H., "Some diseases in the Jewish race," *Bulletin, Johns Hopkins Hospital,* Vol. 43, 1928.

4.   Sorsby, A., and Sorsby, M., "Racial Diseases of Jews," *Jewish Review,* 1932.

Table 1

SUMMARY OF REPORTS OF HIGH AND LOW RATES OF DIABETES

LOW RATES	HIGH RATES
Nineteenth-century sugar cane cutters of West Indies	Many tribes of American Indians
Poor of London and Berlin before 1900	Rich Indian men of Bengal
Eskimos	Many populations of immigrants from India living in various parts of the world
North American Indians before 1940 and in some present tribes	Malta
Jewish Yemenites and Kurds	Uruguayans of Montevideo
Micronesians, Melanesians and Polynesians	Many groups of Polynesians and Micronesians
Algeria	Black women in USA
Morocco	Malays of Cape Town
Rural blacks of Africa south of the Sahara	Many groups of Jews, including Sephardic Jews of Zimbabwe
Poor whites, blacks, and Indians of Central America	Welsh
Blacks in rural USA prior to 1924	Luxembourg, Belgium, and Holland
Belize	Urbanized Australian Aborigines
Bahamas	Mabulag Islanders of Torres Straits
Grenada	Chinese-American men
Haiti, Jamaica, British Guiana (Guyana), and Cuba before 1922	High frequency "legendary" in certain groups, including sumo wrestlers of Japan and royal families of Polynesia and Zululand
Rural poor of India	Mauritius
Broayas of the Sahara	
Chinese and Malays of Singapore	
Philippines	
Thailand	
Burma	
Papua New Guinea	
Rural Fijians	
Republic of Korea	
Viet Nam	
Bangladesh	
Yemen	
Jordan	
Affluent societies during war-related famines	

Source: West, K. M. *Epidemiology of diabetes and its vascular complications.* New York, Elsevier, 1978.

Table 2

DIABETES MORTALITY BY COUNTRY OR AREA

Mortality rate by age per 100,000

Country or area	All ages	35-44	45-54	55-64	65-74	75+
Africa						
Egypt, 1973	6.7	4.3	15.9	38.9	67.2	67.7
Mauritius, 1976	30.1	12.6	68.3	158.5	316.9	391.8
America						
Chile, 1975	10.7	7.3	18.9	56.4	142.0	236.5
Costa Rica, 1975	12.7	3.9	20.7	58.5	155.8	341.4
Dominican Rep., 1975	5.9	4.5	13.5	39.4	62.0	106.6
El Salvador, 1974	4.3	3.8	7.9	26.4	58.1	79.4
Honduras, 1975	2.1	2.5	2.4	10.1	27.8	74.5
Paraguay, 1975	11.0	3.0	15.4	68.7	127.7	217.8
Puerto Rico, 1975	22.0	2.5	13.8	56.8	161.1	393.4
USA, 1975	16.5	4.2	10.3	29.3	75.2	174.3
Venezuela, 1975	11.3	4.8	22.5	72.8	155.6	283.8
Asia						
Hong Kong, 1976	6.5	1.2	5.6	26.6	56.4	90.5
Israel, 1975	7.5	1.7	4.1	16.7	46.2	109.3
Japan, 1976	8.2	2.1	5.5	18.1	54.2	97.0
Singapore, 1976	14.7	3.5	16.9	64.6	182.7	236.3
Thailand, 1976	1.8	1.7	7.3	11.4	16.0	16.2
Europe						
Austria, 1976	15.2	1.5	4.7	16.4	58.8	126.6
Belgium, 1975	34.2	2.9	8.2	34.4	143.8	327.3
Bulgaria, 1976	9.4	2.3	4.6	22.8	50.7	63.4
Czechoslovakia, 1974	17.3	2.6	7.7	33.8	86.7	151.6
Denmark, 1976	12.3	4.4	6.5	15.5	41.8	107.9
England and Wales, 1975	10.4	2.1	3.6	12.0	37.5	93.3
German Dem. Rep., 1976	20.5	1.6	5.7	24.4	81.7	153.2
Germany, Fed. Rep., 1975	35.5	3.0	9.0	39.8	143.6	332.3
Greece, 1975	29.5	2.3	7.6	45.1	143.5	284.2
Hungary, 1976	11.5	1.1	5.0	20.7	56.4	85.6
Ireland, 1975	12.0	1.3	7.0	12.6	63.5	134.7
Malta, 1976	79.2	8.7	28.1	146.4	491.9	1,243.9
Netherlands, 1976	14.4	1.7	7.2	30.2	54.6	165.3
Northern Ireland, 1975	6.3	0.6	2.4	11.0	30.5	67.9
Norway, 1976	7.2	2.0	3.6	6.8	23.3	70.3
Romania, 1976	3.6	1.1	3.1	9.7	20.2	23.8
Scotland, 1976	12.2	2.0	4.4	17.5	45.8	114.2
Sweden, 1976	19.2	6.1	8.2	17.6	57.8	214.4
Switzerland, 1976	17.6	2.4	3.7	15.2	73.3	196.0
Oceania						
Australia, 1975	12.7	2.6	5.8	23.9	70.4	175.8
New Zealand, 1975	15.3	2.8	13.0	32.8	78.3	204.1

Source: *World health statistics annual 1978. Vol. I: Vital statistics and causes of death. Geneva, World Health Organization, 1978.*

Wherever you are, if there has been diabetes in your family, lose a little weight, become more physically fit, develop a healthier lifestyle, eat a more well-balanced diet, stop smoking (if you smoke), watch your blood pressure, and follow your physician's advice regarding good health habits. Your chances of developing diabetes may be reduced. If you do develop diabetes, your chances of controlling it — instead of diabetes controlling you — will be increased.

Ess, gesundterheit! (Eat, in good health)

The fundamentals of good diabetes control are appropriate diet, exercise, insulin or an antidiabetes agent and a good mental attitude. Your good mental attitude includes enjoying what you eat and knowing that your diet isn't really very different from that of other members of your family. Your kosher diet for good diabetes control can be full of variety and choice.

By following the food preparation suggestions, recipes and serving suggestions in this book, you can become healthier and live more happily with your diabetes. And, you'll control your waist instead of letting it control you!

In the next chapter, you will find suggestions for obtaining additional information on living with diabetes and kosher cooking that may be useful to you or someone you love. Also, you will find the Word List helpful in understanding and discussing diabetes control and your kosher diet.

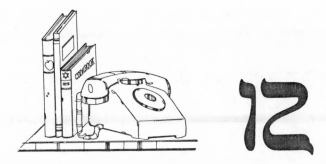

Resources

Many national and local organizations, libraries, and bookstores have resources available to help individuals control their diabetes. Information is provided in easy-to-understand form for consumers and in somewhat more complex form for health care professionals.

You can learn more about diabetes as well as kosher cooking. Your local public library is a good place to begin. Look in the sections marked "health," "diet," "medical ethics," and "religion." Your librarian will be happy to assist you in locating books with information that will help answer your questions.

Bookstores also have many titles concerning diabetes and kosher cooking. Additionally, some books and materials are available for sale through the mail. Watch for book displays in gift shops and synagogues and announcements of new publications in newsletters of various Jewish organizations.

Some books about diabetes

KAHN, Ada P., M.P.H. *DIABETES ("Help Yourself To Health" Series),* Contemporary Books, Inc., Chicago, and Beaverbooks, Ltd., Don Mills; Ontario, Canada, 1983.

LODEWICK, Peter A., M.D. *A DIABETIC DOCTOR LOOKS AT DIABETES: HIS AND YOURS,* RMI Corporation, Cambridge, MA, 1982.

American Diabetes Association, Inc., *DIABETES IN THE FAMILY,* Robert J. Brady Co., Bowie, MD, 1982.

FRANZ, Marion J. *EXCHANGES FOR ALL OCCASIONS,* International Diabetes Center, St. Louis Park Medical Center Research Foundation, St. Paul, MN, 1983.

Some cookbooks for those with diabetes and other special needs

American Diabetes Association, Inc. and the American Dietetic Association, *FAMILY COOKBOOK,* Prentice-Hall, Englewood Cliffs, NJ, 1980.

MIDDLETON, Katharine, and HESS, Mary Abbott. *THE ART OF COOKING FOR THE DIABETIC,* Contemporary Books, Inc., Chicago, 1979.

LEVITON, Roberta. *THE JEWISH LOW-CHOLESTEROL COOKBOOK,* Paul S. Eriksson, Middlebury, VT, 1978.

Some books about Jewish cooking

SHOSTECK, Patti. *A LEXICON OF JEWISH COOKING,* Contemporary Books, Inc., Chicago, 1979.

LONGSTREET, Stephen and Èthel. *THE JOYS OF JEWISH COOKING,* Doubleday and Co., Inc., Garden City, NY, 1974.

Jewish medical ethics

JAKOBOVITZ, Immanuel. *JEWISH MEDICAL ETHICS,* Philosophical Library, New York, NY, 1959.

Information on kosher foods

THE KOSHER DIRECTORY
Union of Orthodox Jewish Congregations of America
45 W. 36th Street
New York, NY 10018
(Annual Passover Directory also available)

KASHRUTH Handbook for Home and School
Union of Orthodox Jewish Congregations of America
45 West 36th Street
New York, NY 10018

THE APPOINTED SEASONS OF THE LORD
(Fundamentals of the Jewish calendar)
Chicago Rabbinical Council
3525 West Peterson Avenue
Chicago, IL 60659

PASSOVER IN THE JEWISH HOME
Chicago Rabbinical Council
3525 West Peterson Avenue
Chicago, IL 60659

For Jewish vegetarians

You may obtain a newsletter containing vegetarian recipes and information about meetings of the Jewish Vegetarian Society (there are chapters in many cities). Write to:

Jewish Vegetarian Society
1265 Westmoor Road
Winnetka, IL 60093

Publications about diabetes

You may enjoy reading about the latest developments in diabetes research and treatment in *Diabetes Forecast,* the journal published by the American Diabetes Association. For subscription information, write to:

American Diabetes Association
2 Park Avenue
New York, NY 10016
Telephone: (212) 683-7444

The National Diabetes Information Clearing House publishes a monthly newsletter. You may request to be on their mailing list. Also, they will send you a free bibliography of books and other materials about diabetes.

National Diabetes Information Clearing House
P.O. NDIC
Bethesda, MD 20205

Information about care of children with diabetes

There is an organization which provides specialized information regarding care of children who have diabetes. Write to:

Juvenile Diabetes Association
23 E. 26th Street
New York, NY 10010
Telephone: (212) 889-7575

More services for those with diabetes

The American Diabetes Association also makes available many books and pamphlets on specialized areas of caring for individuals with diabetes, including the particular concerns of children, summer camps for children with diabetes, pregnant women, taking good care of your feet and tips on traveling (see address above).

The American Diabetes Association, through its many regional affiliates, provides a wide variety of programs for individuals and groups. To locate the affiliate closest to you, contact the American Diabetes Association (see above).

Education for health care professionals

The American Association of Diabetes Educators is a professional organization which fosters and updates professional standards of diabetes education and practice and identifies for the consumer, competencies and excellence in practice within diabetes education and care.

Membership in the American Association of Diabetes Educators is open to diabetes educators, individuals in industry engaged in the production and/or sales of products and/or services useful for diabetes educators, any hospital or medical center with a diabetes education program, and persons interested in diabetes education (that's all of us!).

AADE has local chapters and regional meetings. The quarterly journal is *The Diabetes Educator;* a bi-monthly newsletter is also published. For information, write to:

American Association of Diabetes Educators
North Woodbury Road, Box 56
Pitman, NJ 08071

World-wide services for individuals who have diabetes

At the time of this publication, the author contacted many organizations around the world to determine types of services provided for diabetics. Following is a brief listing of the groups that responded and how readers may obtain information.

Canada

The Canadian Diabetes Association, with affiliates throughout Canada, provides education and research in the field of diabetes. Their official journal is *Dialogue*. Exchange Lists and other instructional materials are available in French, Italian, Ukranian and Portugese.

For information regarding membership in the CDA, details on local affiliates, subscription to the journal and their catalog of educational items available, both medical and nutritional, write to:

Canadian Diabetes Association
78 Bond Street
Toronto, Ontario
Canada M5B2J8
Telephone: (416) 573-4311

The British Columbian Division of the Canadian Diabetes Association has arranged for translation of two Canadian Diabetes Association publications *(Basics of the Diabetic Way of Eating* and *Exchange Lists for Meal Planning for Diabetics in Canada)*. These publications are available in the following languages: Chinese, Japanese, Punjabi, Greek, Portugese and Italian. You may request single copies of these items from:

Canadian Diabetes Association
British Columbian Division
#B-100-1089 West Broadway
Vancouver, British Columbia
Canada V6H2V3

England

The British Diabetic Association is the first Association of diabetics in the world and the first self-help organization in the United Kingdom. There are 300 branches and parent groups through the United Kingdom.

Their publication, *Balance,* issued bi-monthly, is sent free to all members. The newspaper publishes a wide range of items regarding goods, visual aids and information on all aspects of diabetes.

Additionally, the British Diabetes Association produces a catalog of educational books, diet and recipe books, children's books, pamphlets, equipment, identity items and other goods. Write to:

British Diabetic Association
10 Queen Anne Street
London WIM OBD
England
Telephone: 01-323 1531

Australia

In Australia, The Australian Diabetes Foundation is the "parent" organization with many branches throughout the country which provide educational programs and services to diabetics. The Foundation publishes a quarterly journal, *Diabetes Conquest*. Write to:

Australian Diabetes Foundation
27 Brewer Street
East Perth
Western Australia 6000

The Diabetic Association of Western Australia (Inc.) produces a quarterly magazine, *Service,* which is published by the Diabetic Publishing Company of WA. Write to:

Diabetic Association of Western Australia (Inc.)
48 Wickham Street
East Perth, W.A. 6000
Australia

Both *Diabetes Conquest* and *Service* are distributed to members, public libraries and major hospitals.

There are other diabetes organizations in Australia that responded to the author's request for data. All provide information and services for those with diabetes. A few of them are:

Diabetic Association of Queensland
P.O. Box 372
North Quay
Brisbane, Q. 4000
Australia

Diabetic Association of New South Wales
9th Floor, National Building
250 Pitt Street
Sydney, N.S.W. 2000
Australia

For additional information regarding diabetes organizations in Australia, write to the Australian Diabetes Foundation (above address).

Updates of international listings

At the time of publication, many diabetes organizations were contacted but had not responded to the author's request for information. The list of worldwide organizations of interest to diabetics will continue to expand as replies are received.

For details on diabetes organizations not mentioned, please write to the author:

Ada P. Kahn, M.P.H.
P.O. Box 1594
Skokie, IL 60077
U.S.A.

Information about high blood pressure

The American Heart Association publishes booklets and pamphlets on topics about heart disease. The materials on high blood pressure may interest some individuals who have diabetes. Write and request a catalog of their publications.

American Heart Association
National Center
7320 Greenville Avenue
Dallas, TX 75231

Another source of information relating to high blood pressure is:

High Blood Pressure Information
120/80 National Institute of Health
Bethesda, MD 20205

Some items for the visually impaired

You may write to the American Foundation for the Blind and request a free catalog of publications which describes items of particular interest to individuals who have diabetes. Items listed include canes, watches, kitchen aids and devices that enable blind diabetics to measure and administer insulin.

The American Foundation for the Blind
15 W. 16th Street
New York, NY 10011

The New York Association for the Blind records *Diabetes Forecast* (publication of the American Diabetes Association). They also have a list of books and pamphlets available in inkprint and Braille.

New York Association for the Blind
111 E. 59th Street
New York, NY 10022

Other health concerns of worldwide readers

In other countries, the diabetes associations can provide details on where to write for information on heart disease, vision and other health concerns. Please write to the diabetes association and ask for information about organizations in your country which provide specific materials of interest to you.

Some items of interest to travelers

THE JEWISH TRAVEL GUIDE
Sepher-Hermon Press, Inc.
53 Park Place, Suite 503
New York, NY 10007

HEALTH INFORMATION FOR THE INTERNATIONAL TRAVELLER
U.S. Public Health Service
Superintendent of Documents
Government Printing Office
Washington, D.C. 20402

THE NEW TRAVELLER'S HEALTH GUIDE
Acropolis Books, Ltd.
2400 17th Street, N.W.
Washington, D.C. 20009

Diabetic identification

Your physician may advise you to wear some form of identification concerning your diabetes. The identification should provide information which would be helpful for caretakers in case of a medical emergency. A designation that you take insulin can be included on the identification.

You can obtain a bracelet or medallion with your medical information by joining Medic Alert for a lifetime membership fee of $15 (at the time of this publication).

Medic Alert
Box 1009
Turlock, CA 95381

Outside of the United States, local diabetes associations can provide information on obtaining identification materials.

Self-help organizations

During 1984, the Association of Jewish Diabetics, a self-help group, held its first meetings in New York City. The purpose of the organization is to investigate Halachic and medical information concerning diabetes. For information write to:

Association of Jewish Diabetics
1820 East 15th Street
Brooklyn, N.Y. 11229
Telephone: (212) 375-4519

If there is no self-help group for kosher diabetics in your community, write to the New York Association for information on how they went about starting their group. Their experience will be helpful to you and your community.

Also, talk to your rabbi, local community center director or hospital dietitian about gathering together those with similar interests. You can exchange information about products and services for diabetics, coping with diabetes control, recipes for kosher foods, and other aspects of diabetes control and the kosher diet.

There are other self-help organizations and telephone networks that provide information and psychological support to individuals with many chronic illnesses and personal problems. If you would like to learn more about such groups, contact:

The Self-Help Center
1600 Dodge Avenue, S-122
Evanston, IL 60201

or

National Self-Help Clearinghouse
33 W. 42nd Street
New York, NY 10036

Of interest to computer enthusiasts

Computer software (a floppy disc) is available to help calculate diabetic and/or weight control diets and also to calculate the sodium content of meals or foods. Write to:

EBNA (Exchange Based Nutritional Analysis)
Box 34882
Bethesda, MD 20817

Keeping this book up-to-date

The author plans a sequel to this book in which favorite recipes from kosher diabetic readers throughout the world will be included. If you have a favorite dish which other kosher diabetics might enjoy, please share. Send your recipes to:

Ada P. Kahn, M.P.H.
P.O. Box 1594
Skokie, IL 60077

Understanding the words

As a handy resource to explain some of the terms you have found in this book and will see in other literature, the Word List follows.

Word List

Following are explanations of some words to help you understand what your doctor and dietitian tell you and what you read in your cookbooks. Some words pertain to diabetes and other health concerns and some words pertain to foods. If you do not understand these definitions or how they apply to you, please discuss your questions with your physician and your dietitian. A few words pertaining to Kashrut are included. If you have questions about matters of Kashrut, please ask your orthodox rabbi.

Acidosis: An abnormal condition resulting from too high a level of acids in the blood. Sometimes this is referred to as ketoacidosis.

Adrenaline: A hormone in the body that prepares the body for emergencies by raising blood pressure, increasing the heart rate and increasing blood sugar.

Agar agar: Kosher vegetable substitute for animal gelatin found in desserts, candies and frozen dairy products.

Alcohol: Made from carbohydrates and is digested like a 'fat in the body. Beverages such as hard liquor, beer and wine range in alcohol content from a small percent to more than 50 percent. Alcohol provides 7 calories per gram in its pure state.

Amino acids: Proteins are made up of amino acids.

Ashkenazic: This term refers to Jewish people of northern and eastern Europe and their descendants living in other countries. Once it referred only to Jewish people of Germany and their descendants. It is also used to distinguish the Jewish people and culture of the above areas from Sephardic Jews who originated in Spain and Portugal.

Aspartame: A synthetic, low-calorie sweetener (2 calories per teaspoon vs. 16 calories per teaspoon for white sugar). It is composed of two naturally occurring amino acids (building blocks of protein) and is 180 times sweeter than sugar. It is used in some presweetened food products such as powdered beverage mixes and cereals, soft drinks, and is available in stores in its purified form.

Arteriosclerosis: The general term for many diseases of blood vessels; atherosclerosis .is the disease that most concerns diabetics. *(See below.)*

Atherosclerosis: Deposits of fat and other substances in the walls of arteries which cause loss of elasticity and decreased blood flow.

Beta cells: Located in the pancreas and are responsible for producing the body's supply of insulin.

Blood pressure: The force exerted by blood as it is pumped through the arteries.

Blood sugar: The level of glucose in the blood which can be determined by a simple laboratory test or self-tests using sticks or strips.

Brittle: Describes a form of diabetes that is especially sensitive to changes in blood sugar and insulin levels. This situation is sometimes referred to as labile or unstable.

Brown sugar: A form of sucrose containing molasses, which is also a sugar.

Calcium stearol lactylate: Usually non-kosher but may be derived from soy beans and *pareve*. Requires Kashrut supervision; found in instant potato products.

Calorie: A unit used to express heat or energy obtained from food. About 3,500 calories are equivalent to one pound of body weight. Carbohydrates, fats and proteins are energy sources and provide calories.

Carageenen: Kosher vegetable substitute for animal gelatin found in desserts, candies and frozen dairy products.

Carbohydrates: Sugars and starches that are made up of carbon, hydrogen and oxygen. They are a major energy source for the body and provide about 4 calories per gram.

Cholesterol: A fat-like substance found in animals that is an essential component of human cells. When too much is in the blood it sticks to artery walls, clogs them and causes atherosclerosis. *(See above.)*

Chometz: Designates all leavened foods, drinks and ingredients containing wheat, rye, barley, oats or spelt. Certain cereals, breakfast foods, grain alcohol, grain vinegar, yeast and malt products are forbidden during Passover. *(see Chapter 6.)* Legumes (beans, corn, peas, rice, etc.), mustard and the derivatives of these foods are *chometz* to Ashkenazic Jews during Passover. Sephardic, Yemenite or Oriental Jews, however, do eat legumes during Passover. Passover foods containing flour, such as matzos, cakes, macaroons, and egg noodles, require rabbinic endorsement for Passover, as do candy, soft drinks, wines, liquors, milk and milk products, horseradish, vinegar and canned goods.

Coma: In persons with diabetes, coma may result from hypoglycemia or hyperglycemia. Coma is a state of profound unconsciousness.

Corn sugar: A form of glucose made from cornstarch that is about half as sweet as sugar. (Corn sugar is not used in Passover foods.)

Corn sweetener: A liquid sugar that is derived from cornstarch. (Not used in Passover foods.)

Cream of tartar: Kosher derivative from processed wine sediments found in confections and baked goods.

Dextrose: The commercial name for glucose. *(See below.)*

Diabetes insipidus: A disorder in which the body excretes large amounts of urine; the urine is normal and sugar is not present as it is in diabetes mellitus.

Diabetes mellitus: The term was derived from Greek words meaning "passing through" and "sweet as honey." The condition is characterized by an excess of sugar in the blood and/or urine. It develops because the body has an inability to make appropriate use of food as a result of insufficient availability of insulin. In this book, diabetes mellitus is referred to simply as "diabetes."

Diabetologist: A physician who specializes in treating diabetes.

Dietetic foods: Foods for special diets, such as low-sodium, water-packed, or sugar-reduced, are often labelled "dietetic" but are not necessarily intended for use by individuals with diabetes. Check the labels.

Diuretic: A drug that acts to increase the urine output and thus reduces the volume of water in the body.

Dulcitol: A sugar alcohol.

Edema: The swelling of tissues due to an accumulation of excess salt and water in the body.

Emulsifiers: May be glycerides of animal, non-kosher origin; found in baked goods and candies. Requires Kashrut supervision.

Enzyme: Proteins that encourage or hasten a chemical reaction in the body.

Fat: One of three main sources of food energy (the other two are proteins and carbohydrates); fat provides 9 calories per gram, more than double the caloric value of proteins and carbohydrates.

Fiber: Part of vegetables and grains that is not broken down by digestive juices as other food elements are. These are indigestible carbohydrates that are abundant in whole grains, fruits, vegetables and nuts. Fiber is important in the diet because it helps hold water in the intestine, adds bulk to stools and softens them. It also helps regulate the time it takes for food waste to move through the body. (For more information on fiber in the diet, please see Chapter 4.)

Fleishig: Pertains to meat and meat products.

Fructose: Also known as fruit sugar or levulose, fructose is sometimes almost twice as sweet as sucrose or table sugar.

Generic drug: The term used to indicate drugs of a similar class or family. Your physician at times may prescribe a specific drug product by name or may prescribe a generic drug.

Gestational diabetes: Diabetes occurring during pregnancy; sometimes it disappears after pregnancy.

Glucagon: A hormone produced by the pancreas that raises the blood sugar level by causing the breakdown of glycogen (stored glucose). The effect of glucagon is the opposite of the effect of insulin. *(See insulin.)*

Glucose: The form of sugar used by the body for energy; it causes a rapid rise in the blood sugar or blood glucose level. All starches and all sugars break down into glucose, but some take longer than others.

Glucose tolerance test: This is a test done in physicians' offices sometimes as part of a complete examination or when diabetes is suspected. The test involves taking a small specimen of blood from the patient's arm. The test enables the physician to chart the blood's glucose level over a several-hour period. Usually the patient drinks a beverage containing glucose at the start of the testing period.

Glycemia: This denotes sugar in the blood. Hyperglycemia means too much sugar in the blood; hypoglycemia means too little sugar in the blood.

Glycogen: Glucose stored in the liver and muscles for future use.

Glycosuria: This denotes sugar in the urine which can be measured by the doctor and the patient using various home-testing methods.

Gram: A unit of weight in the metric system. One ounce = 28.35 grams. In recipes, gram often is abbreviated as gm.

Granulated sugar: A form of sucrose which is a natural sugar derived from sugar beets and sugar cane.

Halachah: Authoritative code of Jewish religious practice.

Honey: Originating from flowers from which bees collect nectar, honey seems to be a more natural alternative to sugar but is also converted to glucose in the body.

Hormone: A chemical secreted by glands in the body which travels through the blood to stimulate various functions of the body.

Hyperglycemia: High level of sugar in the blood.

Hypertension: High blood pressure.

Hypoglycemia: Low level of sugar in the blood.

Insulin: A hormone produced by the beta cells of the pancreas that regulates the glucose going from the blood into the body cells. In an individual with diabetes, either the body does not produce enough insulin or the cells do not use it properly.

Invert sugar: A form of sucrose which is a natural sugar derived from sugar beets and sugar cane.

Ketoacidosis: In a diabetic whose disease is under poor control, toxic substances known as ketone bodies build up in the blood and cause it to become acidic. Ketoacidosis may lead to diabetic coma.

Ketones: When there is a lack of insulin in the body and tissues begin to break down, ketone bodies form sometimes causing a distinctly fruity breath smell. Ketones are sometimes referred to as acetones.

Lactic acid: Usually synthetically derived and may be dairy or *pareve*; found in pickle products and soft drink flavors.

Lactose: Milk derivative used as a sweetener. Considered a dairy food. Lactose is a combination of two other sugars, glucose and galactose.

Lecithin: Kosher, vegetable derived emulsifying agent found in baked goods and candies.

Mannitol: A sugar alcohol that is absorbed slowly into the blood and causes less of a rise in blood sugar than either sucrose or glucose. In large amounts mannitol may act as a laxative.

Metabolism: The chemical and physical processes of all cells of the body by which food is used for energy and building blocks.

Milchig: Pertains to dairy products.

Molasses: A thick syrup obtained from sugar.

Monounsaturated fat: Fats that are not polyunsaturated or saturated fats; they do not lower or raise cholesterol level. Peanut oil and olive oils are examples.

Pancreas: A gland in the upper abdomen which secretes enzymes into the intestine and contains cells which produce insulin and glucagon.

Polyunsaturated fats: Fats found in vegetable oils which are considered a good alternative to saturated fats. Polyunsaturated fats do not raise the blood cholesterol level. Saturated fats do.

Protein: Proteins are amino acids that are used by the body for repair and growth. Proteins yield about 4 calories per gram. Proteins are one of three major sources of energy (carbohydrates and fats are the other two).

Saccharin: A synthetic, non-nutritive (no calories) sweetener that is several hundred times sweeter than sugar.

Saturated fat: Fats derived from animal sources which tend to raise the level of cholesterol in the blood. Schmaltz is a saturated fat. Physicians often tell people with diabetes or cardiovascular problems to cut down or avoid saturated fats.

Shochet: This is the Hebrew word for a rabbinically licensed slaughterer who kills animals and chickens under strict rabbinical supervision. The *shochet* is a very pious individual.

Sodium caseinate; Milk ingredient found in "non-dairy" products and coffee creamers. Considered a dairy food.

Sorbitol: A chemical substance that tastes sweet but is more slowly absorbed by the body than sugar. Sorbitol, like mannitol and xylitol is a sugar alcohol and in excess may act as a laxative.

Starch: Through digestion starches break down into sugars. Starches do not generally taste sweet. Examples of starches are cereal, potatoes and noodles.

Sucrose: Sugar derived from sugar beets and sugar cane. Other names for sucrose are beet sugar, brown sugar, cane sugar, invert sugar, raw sugar, turbinado sugar and table sugar. You may see these in ingredient lists on canned and processed foods.

Tartaric acid: Kosher derivative from processed grape stems found in baked goods and candies.

Torah: This Hebrew word literally means "law" or "teaching." Judaism teaches that Moses received the Torah, or Written Law, on Mount Sinai. Judaism further believes that Moses received a detailed explanation for the laws which were handed down through the generations; this constitutes the Oral Law which is an integral part of the Torah. The laws about Kashrut and reverance for life come from the Torah.

Traif: A Hebrew term describing animals found non-kosher due to physical damages or imperfections. It is commonly used to describe all foods that are non-kosher.

Vegetable gums: Kosher substitute for gelatin found in desserts and candies.

Whey: By-product of cheese-making process found in baked goods and dairy products.

Xylitol: A chemical substance that tastes sweet but is more slowly absorbed by the body than sugars. Sorbitol and mannitol are similar substances; in excess, xylitol may act as a laxative.

Biographical Information

ADA P. KAHN, M.P.H.

Ada P. Kahn is the author of the "Help Yourself to Health" series of books published by Contemporary Books, Inc., Chicago, (1983). Current titles are DIABETES, ARTHRITIS, HEADACHES, and HIGH BLOOD PRESSURE.

As a health and medical writer, she has worked with many health-related associations and organizations in educational, editorial and promotional capacities during the past 25 years. Her background includes projects with the American Medical Association, the American Academy of Dermatology, the Michael Reese Health Plan and major pharmaceutical companies. She has developed patient education materials, assisted physicians in preparing manuscripts for publication, and served as a consultant to public relations and advertising agencies with health-related clients.

Ada Paskind Kahn has authored more than 75 articles in national magazines including *Your Health and Fitness, Recreation Management, The Apothecary, Medical Record News, Laboratory Medicine* and *Chicago Medicine.* She contributed two papers at national meetings of the Group Health Association of America's Group Health Institute which were published in the Institute's *Proceedings.*

She served as editorial consultant to the U.S. Army Department of Medical History and as public relations consultant to the Office of Health Maintenance Organizations, Region V, U.S. Department of Health and Human Services.

Kahn, a native Chicagoan, received her Master of Public Health (M.P.H.) and Bachelor of Science in Journalism (B.S.J.) degrees from Northwestern University. She has been on the faculties of the Journalism Department of Columbia College, Chicago, and the University of Health Sciences/The Chicago Medical School, North Chicago, Illinois, where she taught courses in public relations and professional communications.

Kahn was named a Fellow of the American Medical Writers Association (AMWA) in 1975. She has taught courses in public relations for health-related associations, medical communications, and free lance writing at eight annual national meetings of AMWA. She is past chairman of the Public Relations Section of the national AMWA organization and has served on its educational and awards committees. She received the President's Award from AMWA at the 1982 annual national meeting. She is a past president of the Chicago chapter and was the recipient of the chapter's Distinguished Service Award in 1979.

She is a past president of the Chicago chapter of Women in Communications, Inc. (formerly known as Theta Sigma Phi), received the Chicago chapter's Distinguished Service Award in 1969 and was editor of the national organization's publication, *The Matrix.*

Kahn is a member of the American Society of Journalists and Authors.

Kahn stays in touch with the public's interest in health issues by participating in the activities of the Skokie Department of Health. She has been a volunteer member of the village's Health Commission for the past seven years and is active on the health promotion committee.

Kahn's interest in writing DIABETES CONTROL and THE KOSHER DIET began while working on her previous book, DIABETES. During discussions with the American Diabetes Association, medical libraries and representatives of the Chicago Rabbinical Council, she found that very little literature was available concerning kosher diabetic patients. "This book will be a much-needed resource for the health care professional who counsels diabetic patients as well as the patients themselves," she says.

When not writing or teaching, Kahn devotes her recreational time to music and sports. She plays the flute and piano and frequently entertains friends with chamber music performances. She is a member of the national organization of Amateur Chamber Music Players. She enjoys playing tennis, jogging and cross-country skiing.

Kahn has one daughter and lives in Skokie, Illinois.

MELVIN M. CHERTACK, M.D., F.A.C.P.

Melvin M. Chertack, M.D., F.A.C.P., is Clinical Associate Professor of Medicine, University of Illinois College of Medicine at Chicago and past president of the Northern Illinois Affiliate, American Diabetes Association.

In private practice in Skokie, Illinois for more then 25 years, Dr. Chertack specializes in internal medicine and diabetes and has a practice limited to diabetes. He points with pride to the baby pictures in his office. "His babies" are those of mothers who were insulin-dependent diabetics during pregnancy and delivery.

"A good doctor-patient relationship makes these successes possible," he says. "Patient compliance with appropriate instructions is of utmost importance in the care of diabetes. We can prescribe and recommend, but it is the patient who must follow through with care at home. Care includes diet and exercise. It is the patient who controls those situations."

Dr. Chertack received his M.D. and Master of Science in Medicine degrees from the University of Illinois College of Medicine, Chicago. He received a fellowship and completed his residency in internal medicine and diabetes at the University of Illinois Research and Education Hospital, Chicago. He was certified by the Board of Internal Medicine in 1953 and became a Fellow of the American College of Physicians in 1956. He has contributed many articles to medical and scientific journals.

Dr. Chertack is now Attending Physician, Department of Medicine, Lutheran General Hospital, Park Ridge, Illinois, and past chairman of the hospital's drug and therapeutics committee as well as many other committees. He is also on the staff of Skokie Valley Community Hospital, Skokie, Illinois.

He has always taken an active part in civic affairs relating to health. In spring, 1984, he was appointed Chairman of the Board of Health, Skokie, Illinois; he has served on the Board since 1960. He has served as a member of the Advisory Committee for Dietetic Technicians at William Rainey Harper College, Palatine, Illinois, as Chairman, Medical Advisory Committee, Niles Township Special Education Committee, and as a member of the Advisory Board, Community Chest, Niles Township, Illinois.

He was honored in 1982 with a citation for public service from the American Diabetes Association and in 1981 received an award for service to the Skokie Health Department from the Illinois Association of Public Health Administrators.

Currently, Dr. Chertack is active in the Northern Illinois Affiliate, American Diabetes Association. He is on the Association's Executive Committee and serves as chairman of the committee on detection. He is a member of the Chicago Society of Internal Medicine and the Chicago Heart Association.

A native Chicagoan, Dr. Chertack grew up in an orthodox home and attended Chicago public schools. As a youngster, he became aware of the high sugar, fat and salt content of many traditional Jewish foods. "*Waist* control has always interested me," says Dr. Chertack. "Now when I counsel kosher patients who have diabetes, I am aware of the results of those traditions. It is hard work to change lifelong habits, but efforts do pay off."

"DIABETES CONTROL and THE KOSHER DIET should help make many patients become more aware that changes can be made without giving up traditional foods," he says.

Dr. Chertack and his wife, Pat, have three children and live in Northfield, Illinois.

RABBI DR. NORMAN BERLAT

Rabbi Dr. Norman Berlat, vice-president, Chicago Rabbinical Council, is Instructor of Jewish Studies at the Hebrew Theological College, Skokie, Illinois, and on the faculty of the College's Seymour J. Abrams Institute of Pastoral Counseling.

He is also a full-time hospital chaplain. He became a Fellow of the College of Chaplains in 1972.

A native New Yorker, Rabbi Berlat attended Yeshiva University in New York City and received his *Semicha* (rabbinic ordination) in 1956 and his Master of Science degree in 1973. He has attended Hebrew Theological College in Skokie since 1975; he received his Master of Pastoral Counseling degree in 1977 and his Doctor of Pastoral Counseling degree in 1980. He is currently a candidate for a Doctor of Hebrew Literature degree.

As a hospital chaplain, Rabbi Berlat is actively aware of the significance of kosher meals in the lives and health of observant Jewish patients. He counsels dietitians, nurses and physicians regarding kosher dietary matters for hospitalized Jewish patients and also works with health care professionals arranging discharge plans for kosher patients. "Food plays an important part in therapy of hospitalized patients as well as those coping with treatment of diabetes at home on an everyday basis," he says. "As it is written in *A Hospital Compendium,* 'the provision of kosher food and observance of Shabbat and holy days as well as general regard for the religious scruples of patients is of inestimable help in the healing process.' "

As a teacher, Rabbi Berlat discusses health matters and diet with theological students who will encounter questions relating to health and diet in the future. "As rabbis, we are aware that the type of food an observant Jewish patient eats is as important to his welfare as the medical treatment he receives. That's why I believe that DIABETES CONTROL and THE KOSHER DIET will be helpful to all health professionals who counsel Jewish patients, as well as to the kosher diabetics themselves," he says.

When not teaching, studying or ministering to the Jewish patients, Rabbi Berlat enjoys his hobbies of amateur radio, flying light aircraft and stamp collecting.

Rabbi Berlat and his wife, Roslyn, have one teenaged son and live in Des Plaines, Illinois.

TEILA FEFFERMAN LICHTMAN, R.D.

Teila Fefferman Lichtman, Registered Dietitian, is Chief Clinical Dietitian, St. Anne's Hospital, Chicago. She has worked as Clinical Dietitian at Bethany Methodist Hospital and as Outpatient Dietitian at Mt. Sinai Medical Center, Chicago. She received her B.S. in Medical Dietetics from the University of Illinois at the Medical Center, Chicago, in 1978.

Teila comes from a kosher home where religious observance was part of everyday life. Her father was the late Rabbi Harold Fefferman. Teila's mother, Rhoda (*bubbeh* to Teila's children), taught her about healthful kosher cooking even before there was widespread awareness that some Jewish cooking habits should be modified. At an early age, Teila developed an interest in food and good nutrition.

Since becoming a professional dietitian, Teila has been active in advancing dietitians' understanding of Kashrut and thus improving the quality of counseling they provide for patients on kosher diets. Teila has given many in-service seminars and prepared instructional manuals for health care professionals on Kashrut and diabetes. She has also counseled diabetic patients in classrooms and individually.

"In addition to being a helpful guidebook for individuals on a kosher diet, this book will be an excellent resource for dietitians and physicians who counsel diabetic or obese individuals," says Teila.

Teila, her husband Heshey (son of Rabbi Oscar Lichtman), and their two young children, as well as their *bubbeh,* were involved for many months as tasters and testers of the recipes and serving suggestions in this book.

Index

NOTES

NOTES

NOTES

NOTES